A FATHER'S HEARTBEAT

Virtues of
Successful Fathers

A
FATHER'S
HEARTBEAT

7
Virtues of
Successful Fathers

RANDAL D. DAY, PhD

Plain Sight Publishing
An imprint of Cedar Fort, Inc.
Springville, Utah

ISBN 13: 978-1-4621-1025-4

Published by Plain Sight Publishing, an imprint of Cedar Fort, Inc.
2373 W. 700 S., Springville, UT 84663
Distributed by Cedar Fort, Inc., www.cedarfort.com

LIBRARY OF CONGRESS CATALOGING-IN-PUBLICATION DATA

Day, Randal D., 1948- author.
  A father's heartbeat : 7 virtues of successful fathers / Randal D. Day, Ph.D.
    pages cm
  Other title: Father's heartbeat : seven virtues of successful fathers
  Includes bibliographical references and index.
  ISBN 978-1-4621-1025-4 (alk. paper)
  1. Fatherhood. 2. Father and child. 3. Parenting. I. Title. II. Title: Father's heartbeat : seven virtues of successful fathers.

  HQ756.D398 2012
  306.874'2--dc23

                          2012004191

Cover design by Brian Halley
Cover design © 2012 by Lyle Mortimer
Edited and typeset by Emily S. Chambers

Printed in the United States of America

10 9 8 7 6 5 4 3 2 1

Printed on acid-free paper.

This book is dedicated to my wife and family.
They have helped me to be a better father.

Contents

Preface   ix

Introduction   1

    The Fathering Journey   2
    How Children See Fathers and See God   6
    Personal Father Interviews   8
    Seven Virtues of Successful Fathers   15
    A Few Assumptions   18
    Types of Approaches Used in This Book   21

Virtue #1: Know Thyself   27

    What's in Your Heart?   27
    Where Your Treasure Is   31
    The Prime Directive—First, Do No Harm   33
    Who Was Your Father?   37
    Research about Father Involvement   40
    Are You Involved?   44
    Becoming "Intentional"   53

Virtue #2: Know the Needs of Others   57

Recent Big Changes in Culture   58
We Can Do Better—Without Going Crazy   70

Virtue #3: Gratitude   77

What Is Gratitude?   82
How Do Researchers Measure Gratitude
    and What Have They Found?   86
Ordinary Savoring: Stop and Smell the Popcorn   91

Virtue #4: Forgiveness   95

Forgiving is a Process   100
The "Affect" Element of Forgiveness   108
The Thinking Element   113
Changing Our Motivations and Behaviors   118
Are You a Forgiving Person?   121

Virtue #5: Sacrifice   125

What Does It Mean to Sacrifice?   127
Applying These Principles   141

Virtue #6: Harmony and Peace   145

Scriptural Foundation for Avoiding Contention   146
The Harmony and Unity Side of the Page   154
Building Harmony and Avoiding Relationship Toxins   160
Teaching Children to Avoid Relationship Toxins   166
Teaching Harmony   170

Virtue #7: Persistence   175

Twelve Guidelines for Teaching Persistence   187
Conclusions   189

Endnotes   191

Preface

THIS BOOK WAS WRITTEN FOR DADS. THE CHOICE TO WRITE specifically for dads doesn't mean I think that mothers are less important in families. Both parents (if there are two in the home) are vital to a child's well-being. However, there are very few books written for dads, especially in LDS culture.

This book was written with the idea in mind that dads can make a difference with their teenage children by embracing their leadership role in the teaching of virtues. The seven primary virtues I have chosen to focus on are to know thyself, know others, and show gratitude, be sacrificing, demonstrate forgiveness, promote harmony, and have persistence. Each of these virtues has been a part of major religious thought for thousands of years and each represents key character traits that, if enhanced, will help a teen be more successful in life.

This book also incorporates research about father involvement. Over the last thirty years or so, there has been a dramatic increase in the attention researchers have paid to the role of men in families. I am one of those researchers and have been conducting research about men in families since the 1970s. I have chosen several key ideas from that research to include here. They are ideas I think can make a difference in the way men teach and love their children.

This book includes stories and pictures from students I have taught at BYU. As a professor, I have taught thousands of students.

Each semester they write family analysis papers and make metaphorical drawings (I call them "Family Flags") that pictorially represent the family they grew up in. Some of those are featured in here as examples of key principles and ideas.

This book also contains data from an ongoing research project that my colleagues and I have been working on since 2005. It is called the Flourishing Families Project. Each year our research team has re-interviewed a total of seven hundred families between Utah County (about two hundred families) and Seattle, Washington (about five hundred families). You will find data examples on each of the topics discussed, as well as exercises to complete that are similar to those we ask our research families to complete. You will be able to compare your responses to theirs.

A primary theme in this book is that children know God first through their parents. The template for how they see God, I suggest, often comes from how they see their fathers and mothers. This book is built on the idea that you as a father have a responsibility in this regard. I am not suggesting that you are "God" to your children, but I do suggest in this book that you will be a more effective parent if you enhance godlike attributes reflected in the key virtues presented here. As you get to know yourself and your family better, and become a more grateful, sacrificing, forgiving, harmonious, and persistent parent, you will be better able to connect with your children and teach them virtues and values that will enrich their lives, as well as your own.

We live in a complicated and demanding world. There are no "silver bullet" solutions for how to cope with that fact. However, the information found here can help us become more involved and more intentional fathers. This book was written with the idea that the fathers who read this book will already be trying their best and want a few good ideas about how to do better. The primary activity of this book helps with that task. I suggest that a key way fathers can have greater influence in family life is to have Personal Father Interviews with their children. This book is built on that notion and provides a step-by-step process on how to make that skill a part of your life.

As you read and use the principles in this book, I would invite you to share your challenges and successes with me. If you have stories, comments, additions, or corrections, please contact me at heartbeatdads@gmail.com.

Introduction: Understanding Heartbeat Fathering

EVERY DAY THE AVERAGE HEART BEATS OVER 100,800 TIMES—
about 2.5 billion times in a typical lifetime. The heartbeat is a
common daily event we don't think much about; hearts don't make
the news until they stop beating. Quality, everyday fathering is
similar. A family's lifeblood flows better when a dad helps with
problems, laughs at jokes, gives hugs for a job well done, sheds tears
when there is pain, provides caring counsel, suggests advice when a
friend has been mean, and soothes the struggles of daily life. This
book is about how men can build a stronger family by being more
involved in the daily heartbeat of family life.

An infrequent heartbeat doesn't sustain life well, which is also
the case in family life. Some fathers mistakenly believe that children
only need to feel their father's presence occasionally. But hearts don't
lay dormant for two or three weeks and then beat like crazy for a few
days. It also doesn't work well in family life for parents to focus their
attention on nonfamily elements of life and then jump in with a good
"quality weekend session." Like a well-functioning heart, family life
is better when dads (and moms) are consistently engaged. In short,
the primary theme of this book is that being an effective father
with teenagers requires rhythmic and continuous effort—much like
a heartbeat. When I mention being a Heartbeat dad throughout
the book, I am referring to this idea—of being continuously and

1

consistently involved in everyday family matters.

Even though the consistent heartbeat is a primary theme of this book, there is an element of the Heartbeat metaphor that doesn't capture how men need to be engaged in family life. In real life, the heart beats as an unconscious function of the brain, and, with regard to fathering, that kind of automatic regularity gives great value to family life. Nevertheless, unlike the heart, effective fathering also takes *conscious* effort and concentration. Therefore, an additional theme of this book is **intentionality.**[1] Men need to be especially intentional and redirect their energy to their families when they feel the world outside their own families is more attractive and exciting.

Consistent and intentional father involvement are the two primary themes of this book. I believe the vast majority of dads do the best they know how and are not basically defective. This book is not a tirade on all the things men should be doing better. Instead, I start with the assumption that dads want ideas about how to do better. This book is not written to try to shame anyone into being a better dad but focuses on what is right with dads.

I need to be clear about the audience for this book. Of course, any of the topics covered here can be addressed to both parents. It is not my intention to state that fathers should be the *only* ones "incharge" of the ideas presented in this book. However, there are two clear reasons I am speaking primarily to dads. First, dads are often the forgotten parent. When you see a "parenting" book in the bookstore, the word parenting in the title is usually a code word for "mothers." I have noticed that men rarely look for books about parenting because they assume those kinds of books are written with a gender bias toward women.

Second, sometimes men believe that getting involved in discussions about parenting "feminizes" them. My experience is that sometimes men are a little uncomfortable reading books about being a better parent. There is a strong cultural push for men to avoid these topics. At any rate, I am glad you are reading it so far and hope you continue.

The Fathering Journey

Several thoughts help define the journey of fatherhood. The illustration below captures the idea that we live in a complicated world where many of us feel that our families are under attack. You may see your teens struggling and your family swaying in the winds of change and uncertainty. The influences of media and culture are strong and often detract from the ideals you hold to be important. One way to counter this is by being an involved father. My belief is that becoming a more effective parent requires a carefully planned effort and a commitment to the ordinary—and sometimes mundane—events of daily life.

You may feel like your castle is under constant attack from the world.

I also realize there are as many different family situations as there are families. Some dads cannot be with their children every day for hours at a time. Some may not have custody of their children. Others may be long-haul truck drivers or corporate tax executives who travel an extended number of weeks during the year. Even serving as a volunteer in a demanding community or church responsibility can tax the time a father has available to spend with his family. So how can we sort through the expectations and complexities and still be effective dads?

One way to begin answering that important question is to realize that there is an ebb and flow in the heartbeat of family life, just as there is in the heart itself. Sometimes the body is resting and the heart beats slowly and calmly. Other times the heart rate is elevated and even racing. In like manner, the work of fathers in families also ebbs and flows. Sometimes fathers work in the background and at other times on center stage. What doesn't work well is for fathers to act as a faintly beating heart, only becoming actively engaged when there is an emergency or a party.

Another feature of the ambiguity fathers feel today comes from our changing times. My grandfather was raised on a farm in Indiana with no electricity, indoor plumbing, automobiles, or airplanes, and was born before our involvement in world wars. Our world is not like his world was. For the most part, our society isn't agricultural; chances are you don't live on a farm and your children don't work with you every morning milking cows and shucking corn. For most of us, those days are gone and are probably over-romanticized. Our time is different. We live in a postindustrial, postmodern, techno-logical age. This is our unique and sometimes crazy era of time. There has been nothing like it in history. But, as Yoda would say: figure it out—we must.

Fathering takes time and effort and can be a daunting task; determining the best fathering techniques in these times is hard. To paraphrase one of my favorite movies, "HARD? It's supposed to be hard. If it wasn't, then everyone would do it. It's the HARD that makes it great."[2]

The research on fathers is only about thirty years old; it's kind of an infant, even, in social sciences. Family science researchers have been much more interested in mothers as they describe what goes on in family life; fathers are difficult to interview, not easy to find, and are less likely to fill out questionnaires. Nevertheless, several family science researchers have pursued the study of fathers and what it takes to become an effective dad.

About thirty years ago, a colleague of mine wrote a ground-breaking essay called "Father, the Forgotten Parent."[3] I thought about borrowing and updating that title for this book. I could have called this book, "Father, Still the Forgotten Parent." I'll bet you sometimes feel like that title applies to you. It seems we only hear about fathers when they have messed something up or aren't doing what they are supposed to be doing. We call this way of thinking the "deficit model of fathering." That is, fathers are frequently seen from a deficit or "what is missing?" perspective. I am going to try to avoid that trap in this book. Instead, this is a discussion of how we can sharpen our skills to do a bit better at the good things we already do.

Today's fathering journey also embraces the idea of role ambiguity. The role of fathers has become more ambiguous in the last fifty years: the description of what fathers "should do" has become less clear over time. Historical researchers tell us that, prior to the 1960s, men's roles were seen more clearly. Men were to provide and women were to manage the children. Today's world is filled with gender ambiguity about which parent should do which tasks and with questions about whether or not the father's role is even important or unique from a mother's. I will try to address each of those topics in this book. My position is that fathers matter, and their contribution in the lives of children *is* important.

In the end, it is problematic when a dad sees his fathering role as unclear and ambiguous. Ambiguity leads to indecisiveness and also promotes distance. If you are unclear what your job is in your family, then you may decide to disengage; or you may choose to take on the role of "older child." On the other hand, you probably know well what is expected of you at work. People naturally spend more time in the areas of their lives where the roles and expectations are clear and, consequently, less time in roles where the job description is messy and unclear.

Still, I believe most fathers try to do the best they know how—and I'll bet your family would say you are a good dad. Nevertheless, if you are like me, being a good dad is not easy in today's world. As your children pass into the teen years, you may have doubts about what your parenting job description is. And it could be that the job you are asked to do in parenting a teenager is more vague, ambiguous, unclear, and even scary than you had realized. It is also possible you believe you have gotten dumber as a parent. Many dads have told me that the older their teenagers get, the more irrelevant and out of touch they feel. One reason we feel uncertain may be that each child experiences life's changes differently. Each time we encounter a teen in the making, it is new territory for them and us.

Another feature of ambiguity is that sometimes a role in life is filled with double or triple messages. Changes in our life course (like suddenly realizing you are the parent of a teenager) are filled with uncertainty. We may feel irrelevant and stupefied because we don't understand what our new role is supposed to be. As our children become young teens and move into young adulthood, we lose our bearing on what we are supposed to be doing as parents. A key goal of this book is to help you reduce those feelings of confusion by presenting seven qualities of effective fathering that will help you identify something specific and concrete you can do with your teenage children.

How Children See Fathers and See God

Fathers have a unique responsibility to represent God in their homes. About twenty years ago, Dr. Mary Ainsworth[4] wrote a paper that has become a "citation classic" in child psychology. In this paper, she developed the idea that children build "inner working models" as they grow. This is especially true for younger children, but it also applies here with children going into the teen years. An inner working model is like a template. Children learn early on, using patterns of life or metaphorical representations, especially about relationships. For example, they pick up quickly if folks they meet are loving and good or not and whether they should trust or mistrust people generally; they begin to know at an early age about how safe or unsafe the world is. Ainsworth speculated that those templates we learn when we are young are durable and don't change much as we get older. In a new situation (like the playground or classroom), children bring that basic template to the new situation. Therefore, if a child learned early that people are to be trusted and she sees the world as safe, she will approach her new classroom with the same assumption; or, if she learned early on that people are not be trusted and she can't be loved, then she may bring those ideas to new situations. Those strongly held inner working models form the ways we treat people and respond to difficulties and successes throughout our lives. Ainsworth thought that those same inner working models follow us into adulthood and rarely change.

Here is my point. How your children see you (from an early age) is a key source from which your children will view future interactions with men (and maybe women also). If they see their father as a person who is interested in them and whom they can trust, chances are they will approach others with that same attitude.

Seeing You—Seeing God. I think this idea is extended to how children see God. Researchers have begun to suggest that how children see their fathers (and mothers also) may contribute to how they view God. In other words, children use the template of how they view parents (especially fathers, I believe) for the way they understand and possibly even visualize God.

The implication of this idea is far reaching. If a parent is harsh, distant, cold, and uncaring, their children may first view God in the same way. We are repeatedly told that God is a loving Father who knows us and cares for us; in like manner, we hope our children see us in the same light.

There is a scripture that helps expand on this idea. In John 13:34–35 the Savior says, "A new commandment I give unto you, That ye love one another; as I have loved you, that ye also love one another."[5] Have you considered how it is that the Savior shows His love for us? One way to think of His love is to remember that He shows mercy, He is forgiving of our many sins, He is there for us whenever we need Him, He teaches the power of gratitude, and He shows us how to build a life filled with unity and commitment. As fathers, we need to model those virtues so our children learn about God's love and compassion through us. In fact, those virtues are the heart and soul of this book. So, I propose that a primary way we teach our children to know God and His Son is by treating our children in the same way God treats us. The first principle of this book states that idea:

Principle #1: As I Have Loved You

Being a successful father means showing the same kind of love to our children that God shows to us.

Elder Richard G. Scott elaborated on the power of the priesthood and how it is to be used in our homes. This quote helps us more clearly understand what our role is as fathers and as priesthood holders.

The purpose of priesthood authority is to give, to serve, to lift, to inspire—not to exercise unrighteous control or force. In some cultures, tradition places a man in a role to dominate, control, and regulate all family affairs. That is not the way of the Lord. In some places the wife [and children] is almost owned by her husband, as if she were another of his personal possessions. That is a cruel, unproductive, mistaken vision of marriage encouraged by Lucifer that every priesthood holder must reject. It is founded on the false premise that a man is somehow superior to a woman. Nothing could be farther from the truth. The scriptures confirm that Father in Heaven saved His greatest, most splendid, supreme creation, woman, to the end. Only after all else was completed was woman created. Only then was the work pronounced complete and good.[6]

This book suggests that we act toward our family members in the same ways our Father in Heaven acts toward us. Further, as Elder Scott reminds us, the Priesthood is given so that we may give, serve, lift, and inspire.

To that end, a primary strategy that will appear repeatedly in this book is the Personal Father Interview (PFI). The following section outlines what a PFI is and how that strategy will be used throughout this book to reduce father role ambiguity, to increase intentional contact with children, and as a way to fulfill our duty to serve, lift, and become the constant and powerful heartbeat within our families.

Personal Father Interviews

I recently heard a story about a young bishop who was approached by the father of a teen. The teen was struggling with several issues, and the father wanted to help. The father knew that one of the issues was the type of thing that should include an interview from the bishop. As the young bishop and the father met to strategize about helping the teen, the bishop was amazed at the close and open relationship between the father and teenage son. The bishop asked the father what his secret was. The wise father told the bishop that the key to the excellent relationship he had with his son was that on a regular basis he had special interviews with his son. The bishop asked about the interviews and what form those interviews took. The father explained that the interviews were informal. That is, they were not designed like a Personal Priesthood Interview or like a temple recommend interview. Instead, these personal interviews were regular—they happened about twice a month—and each interview was (to use Elder Scott's words) about serving, connecting, lifting, and supporting the teen. He went on to say that the interviews were not a platform to give a monthly lecture, nor were they a court session within which the child was judged with punishment metered out.

That story impresses me. I want to capitalize on the wisdom of that insightful father and suggest that a specific way we, as fathers, can have significant and meaningful influence with our children is through regular interviews. I hesitate to even use the word "interview" here because that doesn't quite capture the tone of these special times together. Sometimes we use the word "interview" to connote the idea of a probing investigation. Or we think of a job interview that isn't really much of a dialogue designed to build trust and connection. Its purpose is primarily to find out if the candidate has the right stuff for the job.

Another kind of interview that doesn't work well with our children is the interrogation interview. In this style of interview, the interrogator is probing to discover if the person has broken the law or knows something we don't know. The kind of PFIs I am thinking of in this book should not be interrogations, probing intrusions into a child's life, nor even performance interviews. Of course, we may occasionally want to find out how our teen is doing with regard to certain goals or we may want a worthiness update, but I would suggest that the performance element of an effective PFI should be less frequent than simply having PFIs that build connection, support, love, and trust.

> ## Principle #2: Personal Father Interviews
>
> Interviews and discussions with our children should focus less on performance and worthiness and it is usually not a good time for lectures and administer punishments.

The principle above emphasizes that our effective interviews with our children should be something like the exchanges we have with Father in Heaven. He listens, He is always there to hear our pleadings and problems. He leads us, guides us, and walks beside us, as the song says. His commands are gentle, His yoke is light, and His love is boundless. Sure, there will be a time when we stand before our Maker and account for life. I am guessing that even that meeting will be one of love, concern, and involvement

The following is an excellent example of an effective father interview from one of my students at BYU. As with all the examples I share in this book, the names have been changed and the contributor has agreed to share her story for this book. Not long ago, I asked in class if anyone's father regularly conducted an interview with the children in the family. Of about one hundred students, only seven said yes. I was a bit sad about that, but the 7–10 percent response to that question in the affirmative is about average for the students I teach. One student raised her hand and told the following story about her father's interview style. Here are excerpts from the short paper she wrote about this important part of her life.

Every fast Sunday, there was no need for a reminder: all six kids knew that this was our day for interviews with Dad. I greatly enjoyed my interviews, whether that was because I was going to have more money in my pocket, or I knew I would have a chance to tell him about something really awesome that had happened in my week.

A lot of lessons were taught in those interviews. When I walked in I could feel my father's love immediately and he would always ask, "What's on your mind?" or "What would you like to talk about?" He would then just sit and listen to anything and everything I had to say. I would tell him about school, how my classes were going, what was hard or easy, and how sport teams were doing. I would bring up topics that I did not fully understand, and my dad always seemed to have something insightful to say.

She also commented that this time was devoted to talking about allowances and the use of her money. Her dad taught her about saving money and tithing during these sessions. She concluded with the following:

I love that I had the opportunity to relate to my dad and build the relationship I did with him through these monthly interviews. That relationship now spans two thousand miles. Whenever I have a question or problem, I know my dad will patiently listen to me and comfort me.

Because of those interviews, I feel comfortable telling my dad anything.
That is a special bond that most daughters don't have with their fathers.
Even though he was not always home to see what was going on in my life,
I could still fill him in on the details.

This story captures the essence of how powerful Personal Father Interviews with our children can be. Notice how closely her language about her father resembles how many of us feel about prayer and our relationship with our Heavenly Father. Her father didn't use this time together to lecture (he seemed to focus on the allowances each time—but nothing else was planned), nor did he use the time to judge, assess worthiness, or set specific goals. I imagine that there were times when some of that happened, but this woman remembers these visits as a time for her to share what was on her mind and what was going on in her life.

This book has been designed to help dads become more effective. The stronger heartbeat in a family happens when Dads take the lead in lifting, supporting, connecting with, and becoming an active part of his children's lives. Using interviews as a key tool is an important way to improve your contact with teens and even younger children through using effective PFIs. The following is a summary of how to improve your interviews with your children:

Effective PFIs have **consistency**. The scheduling for PFIs should come from you, as the father. It won't work as well if you don't initiate these interviews and if you don't plan in advance when to schedule them. Notice in the above story that the young woman knew that each fast Sunday was the time for the interviews.

Effective PFIs require some **preparation**. Don't "wing" these. Prayerfully consider the topics to be covered. Take notes about ideas as they come. Listen carefully at dinner times and other conversations for topics that could be covered. But primarily use the time for listening. Listen first—have a backup message to share if inspired.

Follow the **prayer model**. The first element of prayer (besides addressing Father) is to talk about the good things we are thankful for (see the section on gratitude). Our interviews with our children will be much stronger if several minutes are devoted to exploring the good things that have happened during the last week. You may want to include the information on gratitude in this first part of the interview. Additionally, it's a good idea to begin these interviews with prayer. It is important for your child to hear you praying for your family and especially for them.

Here is a list of topics to avoid during a PFI:

Avoid topics in which you are shaming someone or "calling him or her on the carpet." There are times in our interviews for dealing with problems, but if that is the primary theme of these interviews, they will fail. I would suggest that the ratio of listening-based interviews to problem-based interviews should be about ten to one. That is, for every interview that is about suggesting corrections, there should be ten interviews that focus on love, support, lifting hands that hang down, and being a listening ear.

PFIs don't work well when they focus on **compulsion**. Later in the book (Virtue #6: Harmony), I'll explore the idea of compulsion. Compulsion is defined as attempting to get someone to do something we want him or her to do—but that he or she doesn't want to. Avoid this kind of discussion in these interviews.

Also, these interviews should avoid centering on **performance**. Sometimes kids want help with performance, but most of the time they just want us be a part of their life. When you want to work on performance issues (grades, sports, scouting, or young women's achievement goals) schedule another time.

So—what is left? The primary job in these interviews is to **listen** and **pay attention** to the concerns of your teen. Have them tell you stories about their lives (avoid using these times to tell the long and repeated stories of *your* life). Provide a setting where they can express their fears, plans, frustrations, joys, and successes.

Here is an example "plan" for an effective PFI. It is a composite story taken from several sources but captures the main points:

In this PFI, the dad had been taking notes in his journal for several days about Luke's fears. Luke (age fifteen) is getting ready for a class play at school. He was struggling with his lines in the play and the closer it got to the date of the play, the more anxious Luke got. Phil (Luke's dad) noted that Luke was having some kind of trouble with a friend at mutual. Phil heard several off-handed comments about the friend. He also noted that Luke wasn't talking much about his early morning seminary class. At the beginning of the year, there were lots of comments about how great the teacher was and what a good experience the seminary class was.

Phil asked Luke to have a PFI at their regular time on Sunday afternoon. These interviews usually lasted for about fifteen minutes and came before the evening meal, but were scheduled several hours after church. Phil tried several other times, but this one seemed to work the best. Phil wore casual clothes; he decided early on that wearing his church clothes sent a message of formality that didn't match the tone he wanted to set.

Phil and Luke met in a quiet room of the house. Phil made sure to leave his phone in the kitchen, and he told his wife that he was having a PFI with Luke. Doris knew that this was a signal that they needed to have a few minutes together without any interruptions.

The PFI began with a prayer, which Phil asked Luke to offer. Phil didn't have his journal with him. In this journal, he kept some notes about each interview. He decided not to bring the journal to the interview because he felt it made Luke feel like everything he said was being written down as evidence, but Phil did have three or four topics in mind. These ideas had come as the result of reading in his journal from the past couple of weeks, in which he had taken several notes about concerns and ideas he wanted to explore with Luke.

Phil began by asking Luke how math class was going. He chose this topic first because he knew it was a point of success in Luke's life. Luke was very good at math, and Phil and Luke liked to talk about math-related topics. Luke seemed eager to report on his latest tests, and Phil commented on the excellent progress Luke was making. Phil also asked Luke about his Family Life merit badge and how that was going. Phil knew that Luke was only one or two requirements away from finishing it. Phil was conscious about not giving the impression that this meeting was a performance review—instead, he used these examples to demonstrate his genuine concern for Luke's accomplishments and life direction. He also wanted to find out if there was anything he could do to help.

Phil then asked about how things were going in school in general. A lively discussion followed, during which Luke talked about seminary. It turned out that for the last four weeks, there had been a substitute teacher in Luke's seminary class. Luke didn't care much for the substitute and was eager for his regular seminary teacher to return from surgery. Phil hadn't known anything about this development. Phil probed carefully about the sub and the class. There was no lecture or pushing for action. This time together was more about exploring and discussing. This discussion—led primarily by Luke—lasted the whole allotted time. Near the end, Luke asked his dad about how teachers were chosen in the seminary system of the church. They talked for a few minutes about the seminary world. Phil didn't know very much about that but told Luke he would find out and report back.

Phil had several other topics in mind that he wanted to explore with Luke, but their time was up, and it seemed like a good ending. He let the other items go for another time.

Here are some key elements of the story above. PFIs need to be ordinary. By ordinary, I mean that if the only times we have them is when someone is in trouble or needs serious correcting, then the PFIs will never achieve their potential. Who would look forward to going to court once a month (or once a week) to be told all the things he is doing wrong? Instead, the strength of the above story is that the father is using this time to simply connect about the ordinary. Much like daily prayer, we explore the ordinary and daily feelings and events of our lives. When we only approach God during times of trouble, our relationship with Him probably won't be as strong. The same is true with our children. If we schedule interviews only when someone is in trouble, the interview will be more likely to take on a combative and troubling tone.

Each chapter in this book contains PFI suggestions and activities that help fathers build on the ordinary connection with their children. I believe whole-heartedly that Heartbeat dads begin their job of making a difference in their children's lives by strengthening ordinary connections in having PFIs, working in the yard together, building models, and playing games. It usually doesn't happen during the two to three times a year someone decides to get all his fathering done in a big weekend of fishing or snowmobiling. Certainly those kinds of adventures can help, but they will never substitute for the ordinary, consistent, and frequent contact of the heartbeat.

The PFIs are used here instead of promoting the "party dad"

approach, the "Saturday-chore-leader dad" strategy, or the "lawgiver" and "punisher dad" tactic. Shifting your point of view about the kind of dad you are is a key aspect of this book. You should know I am not a fan of the "Disneyland dad" approach to parenting. I have tried it and wished I hadn't. Disneyland dads tend to devote their lives to their work (or hobbies or even church). For some dads, the adventures outside the home are their true passion and love. Occasionally a Disneyland dad decides it is time to give the family a "transfusion" of good will and fun. He wants to take care of his job in one short period of time by trying to give the family a massive transfusion of attention and love during a fun-filled weekend of movies, waterskiing, or some other large-scale adventure. In contrast, the stories and ideas in this book are about dads who are invested in the Heartbeat style of fathering. They know that the lifeblood of family well-being happens every day. These dads know that most of what needs to be done is ordinary and often simple—but takes effort.

Seven Virtues of Successful Fathers

There are seven virtues of successful fathers featured in this book. Virtues are qualities that promote moral excellence. Only in recent years have family scientists turned to the study of virtues as a way to strengthen family life. For many years, researchers have focused on dysfunctions in families.[7] The movement away from only studying dysfunctions, and toward scholarship about positive psychology, is rapidly becoming popular. *A Father's Heartbeat* assumes that you want some ideas about how to do better and not simply a long list of the reasons you are failing. Most of us don't need in-depth therapy to do better, but we could use some ideas to help us do better at being a more consistent and powerful force in our family life experiences.

For example, we are going to talk about how forgiveness is a powerful virtue that is gaining a great deal of attention in family science and psychology in general. This topic teaches us that when fathers learn to be more forgiving, they can better teach forgiveness to their children. Therefore, we examine what it means to live the principle of forgiveness and be a forgiving father, and how to teach forgiveness to our children. Part of authentic love is learning to be forgiving and loving on a daily basis. I found out early that it doesn't work well to go into a child's room and say, "I'm sorry." Sometimes dads think that they can solve problems like the surgeon who puts the defibrillator paddles on the patient and hits the heart with 220 volts once or twice to see if the heart can be restarted. One-shot approaches to forgiveness don't work well either.

I also share real family data in this book. The data covered in this book comes from The Flourishing Families Project (FFP). The FFP is an ongoing research project at Brigham Young University in which we have interviewed about seven hundred (five hundred are non-LDS) families in their homes each year for the past five years. Each year we revisit the same families and try to find out more about how they are adapting to having a child become a teenager. Each of them had an eleven-year-old child when we began. You may want to compare some of your thoughts about family life to their experiences.

Each chapter also features reflections from students in my classes at BYU. I have been a professor in the School of Family Life for thirteen years and in two other schools for twenty-two years before that. During that time, I have collected hundreds of stories and drawings done by students to describe their view of family life. Some students come from families who are not doing well: I am not going to gloss over that. At the same time, I am not going to over-dramatize the negative. We can learn from those who are struggling as well as from those who are doing a great job.

A Father's Heartbeat will introduce you to several principles that form the bedrock of successful and effective human interaction. The new idea here is that many of the good opinions about parenting are rarely translated into how to be a better father. My passion, mission, and approach is to help you become a more effective father using good, solid principles that you already know and use. This book is also aimed primarily at dads who have teens—or have a child about to become a teenager. The principles explored in this book will help you survive and thrive as a dad during those years. The foundational principle of this book is that fathers should first do no harm, and teach children not to harm others.

The following is a list of the virtues and principles featured in this book:

Virtue #1: Know thyself. Heartbeat fathers have learned to take their own pulse and have a clear idea of what they believe. They also know how to turn their own hearts to the things that matter the most, and they know how to teach their children what matters most in life.

Virtue #2: Know the needs of others. Heartbeat fathers have learned how to take the pulse of their family and understand what each child needs.

Virtue #3: Gratitude. Heartbeat dads freely express love by showing kindness and gratitude. They teach the virtue of a thankful heart.

Virtue #4: Forgiveness. Heartbeat fathers appreciate that real love includes real forgiveness. They not only live a life of forgiveness but also teach how to be forgiving.

Virtue #5: Sacrifice. Heartbeat dads understand, live, and teach the power of sacrifice in relationships.

Virtue #6: Harmony and peace. Heartbeat fathers demonstrate how to cope with stress and conflict through living a life filled with harmony instead of contention.

Virtue #7: Persistence. Heartbeat dads are persistent and never give up on their children. They also teach their children to become men and women of grit.

Most readers will experience three kinds of discoveries as they read and complete each chapter: First, some topics covered here will be ones that you already do well with. Hooray for you; that is excellent and cause for celebration. Be sure to write those successes down. Record the positive along with the new things you want to try. Second, you will probably find that there are some strategies you currently use that are not working very well. Like most of us, some things we try don't work well and need to be abandoned. That is a bit harder to do, but learning to abandon strategies that don't work is an important life skill. Third, there may be ideas in these chapters that are new to you. These may take extra effort in implementing. Change in families is difficult and requires focus and effort. Practicing these ideas over several months may be required before any change is noticed.

A Few Assumptions

This book is for dads. As I said earlier, I am writing this book primarily with dads in mind. Moms are welcome to listen in and all of the principles I discuss are important for both parents, but there are so few books written for dads that I have chosen to speak directly to them. Of course I realize that being a father is partly about being a good partner. I hope you don't get the idea that I think men are more important than women in families. Both parents are important and both have jobs to do.

Families are diverse. Some may not have a partner to share their struggles with; others may be going through marital difficulties. I realize not all families have two parents; three charming children who are all above average, have straight As in school, and are all wonderful musicians; a mother who doesn't work outside the home; and no financial difficulties. While a few of you may meet those lofty criteria, most of us struggle a bit more and have lives that are not as neat and tidy. In fact, you may have children who are desperately ill, are not doing well in school, or may not even be interested in making your family better. Nevertheless, this book is about key ideas and principles that should help you become a smarter and more effective parent.

Working with teens. Another key element of this book is that I assume there is at least one teenager or preteen in your family. I don't spend much time here on fathering younger children. However, if you have younger children, this book will help you make that important transition from dad of a younger kid to "wrangler and survivor" of the wild bunch we call teenagers.

I am not a therapist. In this book, I ask you some hard questions about how you see yourself as a father. And I ask you to do some evaluation and comparison about your performance as a dad. Asking difficult questions comes from my training as a university teacher and family researcher. Sometimes my students feel a bit uncomfortable with my probing questions. That's okay; it's how we learn and grow.

I am, however, not a therapist—you should know that about me up front. I work with therapists, I have done some therapy in the past, and I have had some training as a therapist, but that is not the background from which I am writing this book. Therapists typically work with families at the margins. By that I mean they spend their professional lives mostly talking to families that are having enough difficulties that they are seeking out professional help. The vast majority of us are not in therapy and probably don't need to be. But many of us need some ideas and a little help with what to try next. That is the point and direction of this work, and I see that approach as somewhat unique.

The "Principles Approach." This book is not a typical how-to book. It was written to help you know how to use several principles that work. We all have a hard time making the connection between a good principle and how to use that principle. My approach is an attempt to use primarily a principles-based approach and then to show how it can be applied. But that assumes you will also try to find ways of adapting the principle to your own situation.

As I indicated above, this book asks you to be *intentional*. That idea is explored later in greater detail. The ideas and activities presented here require effort on your part—a particular type of effort. That is, being a successful dad requires effort that is initiated by you; it requires effort that is entrepreneurial, innovative, inventive, and designed by you. In my experience, unless a father is taking the initiative to make the connection with his children better, the quality of the content won't matter much. It is like the idea behind self-help dieting: unless the person wants to change and lose weight with all his heart and he is finding ways to do that, no amount of reading and thinking about losing weight will matter much.

So, if you are reading this book looking for a silver bullet quick fix to your parenting woes, this book is probably not for you. As I said earlier, I have been immersed in this field for many years. If there were a magical list of things to do out there, I would have found it by now. Unfortunately, there are a host of authors and motivational speakers who sell the idea that family life can fixed with simple, bumper sticker-like slogans and clichés. You probably know by now that some of those ideas are cute but not very useful.

Although there are no magical lists or silver bullets to solving life's problems easily, that doesn't mean we shouldn't have hope. The "principles approach" used here gives us hope, especially when life is complicated. Here is an example of a silver-bullet approach that needs a bit of rethinking: Conclusive research connecting church attendance and family well-being is spotty at best. There is some indication that religion matters in family life, but the correlation of those two ideas is faint. The principle that we will explore in this book is that unless dads (and moms too) *use* the ideas from religion in family life, going to church doesn't matter much. The silver bullet approach is illustrated in the cartoon below; if you take your family to church, your family gets better. The principle-based approach says that going to church may help you learn how to use certain virtues in family life such as how to be more forgiving, show gratitude, and sacrifice for your family.

Families that go to church together... get strong together ...right?

Church attendance by itself is not a silver bullet to a happier family. Living the virtues you learn about in church, however, is helpful.

Another example of silver-bullet thinking is the "having dinner together" strategy. Sure, having dinners together is a great idea and a potentially useful tool in creating better family life. But if a father (or mother) uses an authoritarian and demeaning style to get folks to have dinner at any cost, there is a pretty good chance that dinnertime will increase family problems rather than lower them. Having dinner is a pretty good overall tactic, but having positive connecting time together (whatever that might be) is a stronger principle that needs to be shaped and put into practice by you (and your partner). So the larger principle in this case would be to find regular times to demonstrate that you care for and love one another.

Getting folks to think at the more abstract, principled level is challenging. Most of us would rather have a recipe given to us and have someone standing by to enforce the recipe. It turns out that teaching people principles instead of force-feeding them recipes is a good general principle itself. So principle #3 reflects that notion.

Types of Approaches Used in This Book

Content. Each chapter begins with some content designed to direct your attention to key principles that will help strengthen your parenting efforts. I have carefully sifted through the mountain of research about fathers in families. From this info, I have picked only those ideas that seem to be well-established and solid findings. This is not a synthesis of all the research we know about a given topic. It was not meant to be encyclopedic or comprehensive. In addition, I have tried to find research I have some confidence in. Research is never about truth and shouldn't be thought of as the final say on anything. However, when we find recurring themes in our research work that make sense, we tend to pay more attention to those findings. I will share several of those finding with you in this book.

Principle #3: The Principles Approach

Dads (and moms) become more effective in their parenting by finding and using good principles of parenting instead of looking only for quick-fix recipes.

Stories. I started teaching family science classes when I was in grad school; for over thirty-five years, I have worked with thousands of students who have spoken openly about their parents. In each chapter, I will draw on their stories and on stories of parents I have interviewed specifically for this book.

Activities. I have been using some of the activities found here in my teaching and research for years. Each activity is designed to illustrate the principles presented in the content parts of the chapters. Please give these activities a try; without the actual practice, the content will have limited impact. The key activity in this book is the Personal Father Interview. I have included at least one PFI example in each chapter.

Data. In each chapter, I will have you compare some aspects of your family life to the lives of families in the Flourishing Families Project. As I mentioned earlier, we have recorded the responses of LDS and non-LDS families about every topic in this book. You will have the opportunity to compare your responses to theirs.

Phone a friend/phone home. I will be asking you to discuss some of the principles and ideas found here with your spouse, a close friend, or even your children. That is the researcher/teacher in me. I believe one way we can find out what our children need is by asking what they want from us. Sounds simple—but it turns out we don't do that well. It is a bit threatening to actually ask someone to give us feedback. Sharing thoughts about parenting can be tough. But talking with a trusted spouse or friend is an important element of the process.

Listening with your heart through strokes of ideas and writing JOTs. I would suggest you keep a "Journal of Thoughts" (JOTs). As I am sure you have discovered by now, most of us have very poor memories. Even when we have really good ideas, the shelf life of that really great idea may last only a few hours or minutes. Unrecorded ideas slip through our fingers like water from the garden hose: it feels cool and inviting for a flash but then is lost. There will be several places in this book to write down what you're thinking about while you are reading.

Strokes of ideas. With regard to ideas and how important they are, the prophet Joseph Smith once said:

> A person may profit by noticing the first intimation of the spirit of revelation; for instance, when you feel pure intelligence flowing into you, it may give you sudden strokes of ideas, so that by noticing it, you may find it fulfilled the same day or soon; (i.e.) those things that were presented unto your minds by the Spirit of God, will come to pass; and thus by learning the Spirit of God and understanding it, you

may grow into the principle of revelation, until you become perfect in Christ Jesus. (*Teachings of the Prophet Joseph Smith*, p. 151.)

Strokes of ideas! Isn't that a wonderful concept? Pure intelligence can flow into us, and we will have "sudden strokes of ideas." That is what I am hoping for in this book. And it is not necessarily the ideas you read here that will be the most important ones. The ideas in this book are like framing a house, making up only the studs and trusses. While the foundational framing is critical, the really important ideas come as you invest in the idea of being a better parent. Those ideas can prompt you. Take those raw ideas and turn that ore into the twenty-four-carat gold strategies.

Your family is so complicated and the history so detailed that there is no way I could really understand it unless I were a part of that system for a long time (a problem counselors face). So, *you* have to do the heavy lifting of translation; I can't do that for you. *You* are the one who is best qualified to make the most difference in your family, and that is especially true if you are willing to listen to the promptings of the spirit of revelation by which pure intelligence will flow unto you. Write down these strokes of ideas or you will forget them.

JOURNAL OF THOUGHTS
Strokes of ideas

This is your first JOT. Record ideas that have come to mind as you have been reading and considering the information up to this point. Perhaps a certain child has kept coming to mind, or perhaps a challenge that your child is facing keeps lingering and reappearing. As you explore and focus on those promptings and strokes of ideas, write down what you are thinking, seeing in your mind's eye, and even feeling. Try to avoid just writing down feelings. While those are important, it is also important to write down what you see as the problem, challenge, or even the strength of a child. As you write, you may find that more of the vision will open to you and you will more clearly hear the child's world, fears, challenges, and needs. These ideas will become part of your first PFI (found following this journal activity).

Teaching as learning. Another way to learn is to teach it. Each chapter has information that should help in building interesting family home evening lessons. I hope you give it a try. I would, however, caution about loading too many ideas into family home evenings. After you read a chapter, think through the principles involved, talk with a spouse/friend, find scriptures and resources you want to add, prepare the lesson well, and then deliver it—in under thirty minutes. I think the best way to kill a good family home evening is to make the lesson too long.

Teaching is more effective when we get past the cognitive part of learning and thinking about the principles, onto *living* the principles. Your children (and spouse) need to see you trying the ideas you are teaching. For example, if you give an excellent lesson on forgiveness and then are disingenuous and unforgiving in your actions—it probably would've been better if you had not given the lesson in the first place.

Your experience reading this book will go better if you try the ideas. Here is a way to get started. As you read the various chapters try to

Sift through the ways you currently father and try to identify how you do your fathering role, why you do things the way you do, and what you want to do differently.

Acknowledge the things you do well and record those as well as the problems.

Honestly **pick** a few things you want to work on and become a more intentional father in your family.

Sort through all of the outcomes you want to see in your children and in family life in general. What do you realistically expect from your children? That exploration is a key activity that has dramatic results.

Synthesize the information into your personal life. Only you know how to implement the ideas found here.

Strategize. Becoming an intentional and directed father is a key idea. This book is not meant to be a "thought shop;" it is more of a workshop that requires action.

The following is the first outline for an effective Personal Father Interview. It is designed to get you started with the idea of meeting with and getting to know your child(ren) better. Try it. I think you will find it a powerful and useful tool.

PFI: The Beginning

1. The PFI is a key element of this book. Begin by finding a notebook or use your current journal. For one week, write down any "strokes of ideas" you have about the target child for this activity. If you have more than one child to interview, have a different page for each.

2. Use the ideas you listed in the JOT in prayer. Like the prayer role of the temple, you can pray specifically for your children in specific ways. Remember that a powerful PFI is not necessarily a time for lectures, admonishments, judgments, or performance evaluation. Instead, it is primarily a time for understanding and learning about your child's world.

3. I would suggest that you not "announce" this as a new program to anyone. Just try it without announcement. Announcements to programs are often met with resistance.

4. Think through the time and place carefully.

5. If your child doesn't want to schedule it, then go with a more informal time like a lunch date on a Saturday.

6. Use this first session to simply explore what is going on in your child's world this week. What are the topics they are focusing on? What are their problems?

7. Take notes after the PFI in your journal. It will be important to note over time how the topics change and evolve.

Virtue #1: Know Thyself
Heartbeat Fathers Focus on What Is Important

All men should strive
to learn before they die
what they are running from, and to, and why.
—James Thurber

ELDER LOREN C. DUNN ONCE TOLD A STORY ABOUT HIS DAD. He related how his father, then a stake president, lived on a small farm and wanted his boys to learn how to work and to build a sense of responsibility. To accomplish this goal, he put the boys in charge of raising the small dairy herd. Of course, the boys made mistakes, and the milk production was not the best. A well-meaning neighbor complained to the father about the mistakes and provided a number of suggestions for how the boys could do better. "Jim, you don't understand," President Dunn explained, "You see, I'm raising boys, not cows."[8]

This story touches me deeply. This story asks each of us to pause and ask the question, "What is it we are trying to accomplish in life—specifically, what are we trying to accomplish as we raise our children?" As we honestly examine our lives, it becomes easier to assess core beliefs about fathering and family life in general. That kind of thinking can be a little scary, but don't pass it by; it is critical to becoming more effective as a dad.

What's in Your Heart?

Think for a minute about what is in your wallet. Take a peek at the contents. What do you see? Now think about the stuff that is in your garage, basement, storage rooms, and attic. It is easy to make the case that what we value the most is kept closely at hand.

The things we believe in the most will show up in our wallets, hang on the walls of our garages, be stored in closets and drawers, and be displayed proudly at work. Archaeologists claim that the stuff people and treasure are telling clues about what people worship and believe to be important. Imagine for a minute that all of the people in your neighborhood disappeared suddenly and your dwellings and your "stuff" was all kept intact but buried for two thousand years in ash like at Pompeii in Italy. When the archaeologists of the future finally uncover your house, they would begin to piece together your life from those pieces and fashion a story about what you believed in, what you thought about the most, and what your life was like on a daily basis.

The first principle of this chapter addresses the idea that the stuff we treasure and display on our walls is an excellent window into what we believe in, not just what we claim to believe in.

Principle #4: The "Stuff" Principle

The stuff we store and display on our walls and how we allocate space and use our time are all key windows into what we really believe in. Those objects are the symbols of our personal core ideology.

In other words, our stuff is a window into our deeply held ideology. The term "ideology" points us to the root word "idea." What is your idea or ideology of life? What is your core idea about children, families, and how to treat a spouse? Where do those ideas come from? Which ideas are better than others? Which ideas work for you and which are just broken-down, worldly ideas that have little fruit to bear?

We can extend that thought and continue the search for your ideological core by looking at how you spend your time and what you spend money on. Wouldn't you agree that taking all of these observations together (such as what's in your wallet, what's hanging on your walls, what's stuffed in your closets and drawers, and how you spend your time) is a pretty good assessment of what you really believe in? It is hard to escape the logic of that argument.

Could we convict you? Now for a moment, consider how fathering fits into the mix. If you examine your stuff, time use, what is on your walls, and what is in your wallet, is there evidence that you are committed to being an involved dad? And what is the proportion of time spent and resources used on your children versus the other roles and commitments in your life? If we listened to your prayers and your private conversations with your spouse, could a jury "convict" you of being interested in your children?

Before we continue, I would like you to do a short writing assignment. Take about ten to fifteen minutes and complete the JOT called "What's in Your Heart?" Taking the time to have a good chat with yourself about your devotion to fathering is a critical step in becoming an effective father.

The JOT found below asks you to evaluate what you think of yourself as a father, where that role lies in relation to the other roles you have (worker, church member, lover, bullfighter, trumpet player, roller-derby coach, and so on). Are you comfortable with the role of dad? Do you really want to be a dad? What do you like about being a father, and what do you not like? Finally, a key purpose of this chapter is for you to record what you think is the key purpose of being a father.

JOURNAL OF THOUGHTS
What's in your heart

Write about Principle #4. That principle asks you to assess how the fathering role stacks up when compared to the other commitments you make in your life. The simple idea is that we spend the most resources on the things we value the most. Given that, how much do you value the role of the father? Of course, most of us think the father role is important. In this JOT, evaluate how much of your thoughts, time, resources, and energy are spent on the role of dad compared to the other parts of your life.

_____

_____

_____

_____

_____

_____

_____

_____

_____

_____

_____

_____

_____

_____

_____

_____

_____

_____

Where Your Treasure Is

As you may have guessed, the primary virtue this chapter is built on is captured in a brief scripture found in the Sermon on the Mount. All of the primary religions ask us to understand what our core beliefs are and then align those beliefs with a higher purpose in mind. A "higher purpose" implies moving away from individualism and moving toward concern for others, including a focus on one's community and world. An individualistic focus begs us to only consider our own needs and wants and to spend less time thinking of the needs of others.

In the simplest and most direct way possible, the Savior says, "Where your treasure is, there will be your heart also."[9] He is asking us to treasure something greater than our own immediate self-interest and consider treasuring the eternal instead of the mundane. I am proposing that to be a more effective Heartbeat father, you should take your first step by evaluating what you really believe to be important. The foundational virtue of understanding who we are and what masters we serve is key. Our core ideology is the fountain from which comes most of the rest of who we are and what we spend our time, talents, and financial resources on. If fathering is a pale, secondary element in dad's life, it is less likely that he will deeply invest in his children. If his core ideology centers on the worth of being a Heartbeat father then he will become much invested in the well-being of his children.

Elder Neal A. Maxwell described the above idea in the following way,[10]

Actually, everything depends—initially and finally—on our desires. These shape our thought patterns. Our desires thus precede our deeds and lie at the very cores of our souls, tilting us toward or away from God (see D&C 4:3). God can "educate our desires." Others seek to manipulate our desires. But it is we who form the desires, the "thoughts and intents of [our] hearts" (Mosiah 5:13).

He continues by noting that,

The end rule is "according to [our] desires ... shall it be done unto [us]" (D&C 11:17), "for I, the Lord, will judge all men according to their works, according to the desire of their hearts" (D&C 137:9). One's individual life will thus remain uniquely his. God will not override it nor overwhelm it. Hence we'd better want the consequences of what we want!

Principle #5: The Desires of Our Heart Principle

From the desires of our hearts—our core ideologies— come our actions. And, conversely, our actions are a reflection of the true desires of our hearts.

Correlate to Principle #5:
The Two Masters Correlate

You cannot have two masters or two competing ideologies. And you cannot be void of an ideology.

Another Correlate to Principle #5:
The Fathering Correlate

Your ideological core shapes the kind of father you are and how much effort you put into that role.

The logic and power of the above principle is inescapable. The Sermon on the Mount also gives us the inevitable correlate: that one cannot serve two masters (Matt. 6:24). Notice how that scripture leaves no room for having no master: inevitably we will serve something or someone, be it a cultural trend, a political ideology, a hobby, our work life, or following and worshipping cultural idols and sports heroes.

The second correlate seems just as inescapable; once we know what a person truly worships—whatever that might be—we can tell a lot about the choices he will make with regard to fathering: in other words, the kind of father one becomes (or will become) is, in great part, dictated by his ideological worldview.

The Prime Directive—First, Do No Harm

From our core ideological orientation comes our ideas about what makes a good father and what his job is. The following section asks us to consider that idea by asking about your parenting style. Part of the exploration asks us to consider if how we parent our children potentially creates good or sometimes leads to harm.

Some possible fathering styles. The job of parents, and fathers in particular, can be illustrated in several ways. What image comes to mind when you think of fathers? Here are some possibilities: One option is that a dad could think of himself as a drill instructor. The drill instructor's job is to train his troops. It is often stated that the first job the drill instructor does in basic training is to strip the candidates of their individuality, remove their sense of being civilians, and then reshape them so they become part of a squad that acts upon orders without pause or contemplation. How close is that idea to what you think a dad should be?

There are some dads who approach parenting with a drill-sergeant approach—I personally don't think it works very well. The basic premise of being a drill-sergeant is that you believe your children are ultimately an ongoing part of your family operation and you are the king of the castle. Our culture and society has moved away from that idea. This approach expects that children will be an appendage of all we do until we die, much like what was expected in medieval times.

The goal of the drill sergeant is to shape the person into something we need to help run our squad or castle. In my opinion, a more workable metaphor for parenting is that our job is to teach our children to build their own castle. We want them to move on and create their own worlds. If anything, our job as fathers is to work ourselves out of a job and turn the keys of children's lives over to them at the appropriate age. Effective dads recognize and build their children's skills and qualities and help them become who they are.

A second parenting style option is the sculptor father. I think we do some harm when we think our job is to carve a child into a copy of us or what we wished we were. The sculptor father believes he has been given a block of granite and his job is to chisel a child out of the stone—a magnificent statue like Michelangelo's *David*. Instead, our job is to discover, counsel, and stand at the side of our children as they become what they choose.

Think for a minute about Lucifer's suggestions in the war-in-heaven chapters in the Pearl of Great Price.[11] Lucifer was part drill sergeant and part sculptor. He had a vision of how people should turn out; he would sculpt the whole piece of art, and he would then take the credit. The other plan was that God's children would choose for themselves who they would become—not the drill sergeant approach and no chiseling. God would stand by and be of counsel, give us good ideas, help as He could, be forgiving, sacrifice, and fill us with love for our good choices. Remember, this one truth is given, "God will force no man to heaven."[12]

Know then that ev'ry soul is free,
To choose his life and what he'll be;
For this eternal truth is given,
That God will force no man to heaven.

Surely that song can refer to our children as much as our neighbors. Instead of being a drill sergeant or sculptor, I think a Heartbeat dad is more like a gardener. He waters and keeps the weeds and rabbits out. He prunes and tends the tender plants in the heat of day and protects them from the cold of frost. He doesn't try to smash a pumpkin into a tomato, nor does he show his disgust and disappointment if a corn stalk is a bit short or a potato plant doesn't produce exactly what he thought it should. Like God, the successful dad works in his vineyard, is persistent in his efforts, takes care of it with pride, and does what he has to do to protect it.

That leads us to the idea of doing no harm. As the gardener, counselor, protector, and presider in a family—there is a Prime Directive I suggest for all fathers. That directive is captured in the Physician's Oath. A key principle of the Hippocratic Oath is that a physician will, "first, do no harm." The same applies to fathers and mothers. The pledge every father should make to his family with all of his heart is that he will first and foremost do no harm. We will return to this idea in the chapter on harmony and contention, but it is also worth stating here. Some men have been and continue to be ruthless in family life. A few fathers are not only deadbeats but they are also physical and emotional bullies.

In summary, becoming a successful dad requires your best efforts.

A successful dad seeks to build his family's well-being through thoughtful, positive involvement. He also takes the solemn oath to do no harm. The joy we feel from being an engaged dad is filled with wonder.

Principle #6: Foundation of Successful Fathering

First, do no harm. Men should be lovers of peace and respect their wives and children with dignity and love. Harming children and spouses in any way defeats the purpose of family life and offends the Spirit. We harm children when we treat or think of them as our slaves, our chattel, or as lumps of stone and that our job is to carve children into an image of ourselves.

You may be saddened if your teens don't make the choices you want for them. But at the end of the day, your only choice is to follow the lead of God Himself and to teach, counsel, love, persist, forgive, sacrifice, and show kindness and love unfeigned. If you use domination, control, or other forms of unrighteous power to try to make your children do things they don't want to do, the results will be catastrophic.

JOURNAL OF THOUGHTS
Doing no harm

Record your thoughts and feelings about this lesson and how it applies to your family situation. What are the corrosive elements in the world that impact your children? How can you devote your best efforts to becoming a more effective father? How can you better take the pulse of your family so you can provide the consistent influence your children need?

Who Was Your Father?

One possible way to uncover what you believe about your family and the role that men should play is by considering your father. Who you are now is, at least in part, connected to the men in your life when you were young. Was your father the lawgiver and disciplinarian? Was he the one who introduced you to the world outside the home? Perhaps he was just another one of the children. Maybe he wasn't there at all and the lesson he sent you was that his presence didn't matter very much. Take a few minutes and write down the first thoughts that come to mind about your dad. Don't write down what you wished he were like. Try to get past the mythology of what is told about him. Honestly tell your own private version of who your dad was to you. This activity can be a difficult one for most men. It can be hard to step back and honestly evaluate what type of father your father was and how you feel about that as a father yourself.

Activity: Who's Your Daddy?

Part 1

Everyone has a father, and some of us have dads. The person who was your dad may not have been your biological father, but for many of us it was. Whatever the case, the first job in this activity is for you to simply identify important men in your life. These men include your social father that connected with you, loved you, maybe hated you, taught you, and—hopefully—cared for you. While it may be that you have no one, there is most likely someone who you can comment on.

List the names of the men who were dads to you.
Your primary social father (this is not always one's biological father—instead think of the person who was in your youth the most as a father): _____

Who were the other men who significantly influenced your life?
_____
_____

Part 2

Write down five things that your father did that helped you become a better person. Then list five things (if there are five) he did that were not very helpful—things you wish he had done better.

Things your primary father did well:

Things your primary father did that were not helpful:

Part 3

Now spend a few minutes and comment on other men who have been influential in your life—those you listed in part 1. Again, take a few notes and then write down five things that your father figures did that have made you a better person. Then list five things they did that were not very helpful—things you wish they had done better. Things other men in your life did well:

_____

_____

_____

_____

_____

Things other men in your life did that were not helpful:

_____

_____

_____

_____

Part 4

This one may be a bit more difficult. Talk with your spouse (or a close friend) and do the same type of analysis about the men in her life. Asking others about their family life experience may be uncomfortable for you, but it will pay off.

Things your wife's (or friend's) father did well:

_____

_____

_____

_____

Things your wife's (or friend's) father did that were not helpful:

_____

_____

_____

_____

Part 5

Finally, what did you learn about yourself as you thought about your father and other men in your life? How about as you interviewed your spouse or friend? How did these men shape their lives? What is it about their approach that shapes how you father—for better or worse? What would you change about your fathering that comes from these men? What elements of their fathering do you want to retain?

_____

_____

_____

_____

_____

_____

_____

_____

_____

_____

Research about Father Involvement

You may be wondering if being an actively involved father really matters. For about forty years, researchers have been collecting a mountain of data that can be summarized in the simple principle below.

Principle #7: Fathers Can Have a Huge Impact

A good father is worth more than
a hundred schoolmasters.

—George Herbert, Welsh poet

The implication of Principle #7 is, however, that in order to be worth more than a hundred schoolmasters, we have to spend the time and make the investment. A hundred schoolmasters (if they are any good at all) would be spending time pondering, planning, preparing, and delivering the best they could. We as fathers need to do the same if we expect to be effective. The following is a short report of several key research findings that show fathers do matter.

The EAR model. Researchers have suggested that father involvement contains several parts.[13] The first part is *engagement* (the "E" part of the model). Engagement is an easy idea to understand, but it is difficult to measure. Engagement is usually defined as the amount of time and energy a father spends benefiting his child. For example, sometimes in our research we ask fathers to keep track of all the activities they do during a day. Researchers then count how many hours a father reads to, plays games with, talks to, or watches TV with his child, or takes his child to an activity.

We may also ask about the quality of engagement. For example, we could ask if you spend time teaching your child something, and we might follow up with questions about how well the activity went: Did you have a pleasant time interacting with your child? Do you think your efforts were well received? Early on in our research about fathers, we were more interested in basic care issues[14] and whether or not the dads were doing the same kinds of things mothers were doing. We are now much more interested in knowing about the quality of children's involvement or engagement with their fathers.

The second part of the EAR model of fathering is *accessibility*. This idea asks how available, reachable, and open fathers are to spending time with their children. Some fathers are very open and accessible, while others are unavailable either physically or emotionally. Here is a quote from a father I know talking about his father.

I can count on one hand the number times my dad was ever a part of my life. I remember one time when I was twelve, I was trying to put a train set together I had gotten for Christmas. In the basement, I found an old scrap of plywood and was trying to nail the railroad track to it. My dad saw me and said, "What are you doing there, lad? Looks like you need a better board." He then told me he would bring a nice piece of plywood home from work the next day. It never happened, and I knew better than to ask about it—there would have been serious consequences for suggesting to him that he forgot something.

We learn from our research that children who find their fathers to be accessible are much better adjusted to the challenges of life and have an enhanced sense of well-being. There will be more on those findings later.

The third aspect of the EAR model is *responsibility*. This is a more difficult idea to use in a research project. To assess responsibility, we want to know if fathers make sure their children are taken care of and are safe, and if men are providing economically for their children. Do fathers put the needs of their children before their own wants? While breadwinning and provisioning is a critical activity, being responsible goes well beyond just putting bread on the table. It means that as teens get older, the father is willing to take responsibility to see that they are careful on dates. A responsible father makes sure teens have the right kind of knowledge to do well in their world. And a responsible father takes the time to demonstrate to each of his children that he cares for them by taking the time to appropriately monitor their activities. As we will discuss in later sections, that doesn't mean intrusive over-monitoring that results in the teen remaining a helpless child. Instead, being a responsible father means he is there as a bridge to the scary adult world.

Findings. When fathers are more involved—engaged, accessible, and responsible—their children do better. Of course, not all children will thrive and survive even when their fathers are highly involved, but father involvement matters in children's lives. Here are some recent examples of research about the value of father involvement.

In 2010, an important study[15] showed that how children view and cope with conflict was directly related to parent behaviors. In particular, father attachment and accessibility was directly and powerfully related to children feeling secure and expressing less self-blame about life's problems. These researchers also found that when fathers were supportive and accessible to their children, when conflict occurred between the two parents, it was not nearly as problematic in children's lives as when the father was less accessible.

"Thanks, Pop, but today's kids don't want money, they want leadership."

In one study I published with my research colleague Dr. Laura Walker,[16] we found that fathers' (but not mothers') lack of connection and engagement with their children was directly associated with adolescent depression and acting out behavior (such as smoking or getting arrested). This study used the same measure of involvement scale found in the upcoming activity. We are publishing more articles using these data, and our findings also show that these trends hold true as children get older. While, father involvement tends to drop as the child gets older when fathers stay involved his influence remains a powerful force in predicting positive outcomes for children.

In a different type of study completed by Patricia Schacht, Mark Cummings, and Patrick Davies at the University of Notre Dame, it was found that fathers who reported problem drinking were more likely to also report depression and increased levels of marital conflict, and their children were directly influenced by these events. They followed more than two hundred families for three years and found that problem drinking in a father decreased his ability to attach to his children. The result, as you would expect, is that those children reported increased depression and thoughts of suicide; were less adjusted, more withdrawn, and more anxious; and reported much more self-doubt.

Why focus on these results? These studies help us understand why being involved in our children's lives is not just a "nice" thing to do or that it simply fills a social norm that describes something we should do. Instead, a mountain of findings, like the ones above, clearly show that dads matter for the well-being of children. The next segment asks you to continue your assessment of how involved you are in your children's world. Again, the idea is that what you believe will lead to action.

Are You Involved?

The next part of this exploration asks you to compare your involvement with about five hundred other men. I am going to have you fill out a short questionnaire about your level of father involvement and then compare your score with fathers in the Flourishing Families Project.

Activity: Are You Involved in Your Children's Lives?

Part I

The following activity uses a short questionnaire that we use in our research. It measures father involvement. Thousands of men have taken this short questionnaire over the years. There is a problem with this type of research; we call this problem "social desirability." This questionnaire assesses how involved you are: Nobody likes to score low on a questionnaire and be labeled a loser, right? So, one way to cope with socially desirable answers is to take this questionnaire in private. Knowing that no one will be looking at it may help you do better at not over scoring.

Here are the questions.[17] Read each one and give yourself a score. A score of 1=never do this; 2=rarely do this; 3=sometimes do this; 4=often do this; 5=very often do this. How often do you:

_____ Attend your child's activities (like a soccer game or something at school)?

_____ Read books or magazines with your child?

_____ Give encouragement to your child?

_____ Take care of your child (like fix him or her food)?

_____ Act as a friend to your child?

_____ Work hard to pay for things your child needs?

_____ Help your child with homework?

_____ Make it easy for your child to talk to you?

Part 2

Now we are going to do the same thing—only with your spouse, partner, or good friend. As before, if you are a single dad, you will have to adjust your numbers and take into account the time you have available.

Instructions to spouse or friend:
This questionnaire assesses how involved _____ is as a father. Please be honest; the power of this assignment is based on having accurate feedback.

Here are the questions. Read each one and give _____ a score. A score of 1=never does this; 2=rarely does this; 3=sometimes does this; 4=often does this; 5=very often does this. How often does _____:

_____ Attend his child's activities (like a soccer game or something at school)?

_____ Read books or magazines with his child?

_____ Give encouragement to his child?

_____ Take care of his child (like fix him or her food)?

_____ Act as a friend to his child?

_____ Work hard to pay for things his child needs?

_____ Help his child with homework?
_____ Make it easy for his child to talk to him?

Part 3

Once you have scored each of the eight items, add them up. You should have a score that ranges between eight and forty.

Take your total score and divide it by eight to get an average.

Now compare that average score to the following data taken from the Flourishing Families Project. In the FFP, there were 341 non-LDS men who took this survey. We started out with 500 families, but 159 of those families were single-parent families with no dad present. The dads' scores look like this:

Score	Number of Men	Percent
1–2	1	.01
2.1–3.0	15	.04
3.1–4.0	153	.44
4.1–5.0	156	.46
over 5.0	16	.05

Group average = 4.07

Here are the scores for the 158 LDS fathers who answered our survey. They are also part of the FFP, but they live in Utah.

Score	Number of Men	Percent
1–2	0	.00
2.1–3.0	4	.03
3.1–4.0	80	.51
4.1–5.0	75	.47
over 5.0	0	.00

Group average = 4.00

JOURNAL OF THOUGHTS
How involved are you in your children's lives?

You are now armed with some data and ideas about what it means to be involved in a child's life. After reviewing your scores on the involvement scale (both your scores and your partner's score of you) and considering the informal assessment of what you spend time and other resources on, fill in the following:

Engagement
Overall, how engaged are you in the lives of your children?

_____

_____

_____

If you have more than one child, are you involved in some children's lives more than others? Explain how that happens and why.

_____

_____

_____

_____

What are some of the ways you are engaged? Be as specific as possible.

_____

_____

_____

_____

Name four ways you could be more engaged:

1. _____

_____

2. _____

3. _____

_____

_____

4. _____

_____

_____

Accessibility

How accessible would your children and spouse say you are in the family?

_____

_____

_____

Write a paragraph or so about a very accessible father you know. What does he do differently (if anything) than you?

_____

_____

_____

_____

_____

Can your children come to you for help as well as for a good time?

_____

_____

Do you feel like they can approach you with confidential information?

_____

_____

_____

Write a paragraph about the last time one of them came to you and comment on how it felt and how the conversation went.

_____

_____

_____

_____

_____

_____

_____

_____

_____

What could you do to become more accessible (if you feel you need to)?

_____

_____

_____

Responsibility

Overall, how responsible are you in the lives of your children?

_____

_____

_____

If you have more than one child, do you feel more responsible for one or some of your children than the others? Explain how that happens and why.

_____

_____

_____

_____

What are some of the ways you are responsible? Be as specific as possible.

_____

_____

_____

_____

Name four ways you could be more responsible:

1. _____

_____

_____

2. _____

_____

_____

3. _____

_____

_____

4. _____

_____

_____

Does your partner see you as responsible? Explain.

_____

_____

_____

Activity: Making Plans

The goal of this activity is to make some specific goals about being more involved. With all of the information from above, choose from the following possible activities or create your own. The goal is to increase your father involvement and become more invested in your children's lives. Be specific about those goals. These activities will help you prepare for the Personal Father Interview at the end of this chapter.

Engagement

○ Thinking and praying: One way fathers can become more involved (engagement) is to do more thinking about their children. How to do that is the question. You could set a goal for the next two weeks of trying to remember each day to spend even five minutes thinking or praying about the needs, wants, wishes, and challenges of each of your children. Be sure to record in your journal what you are thinking about. Changing or altering an ideology means altering what we think about and how we spend our time.

○ Another way to remember to invest in our children is to put pictures of them in our wallets, on our walls, and at our places of work. Walking past those pictures will remind us of our need to think and pray about them.

○ Consider developing a prayer roll. In the temple there is a prayer roll to help us remember those who we are asking special help for. One way to move that activity to the family level is to develop prayer or thought rolls in your journal about specific challenges and needs you see in each of your children.

○ With the prayer roll in mind, spend specific time praying for each child and your spouse as she works with each child (and with you).

○ Cab Driver—Plan during the next two weeks how you can be more involved in picking children up or delivering them to and from lessons, school activities, work situations, doctor appointments, or other events that require giving rides.

Accessibility

○ Make yourself available when your children are at home by turn-ing off your cell phone or favorite TV program and coming out from behind your book or hobby project. Sit near them while they are doing their homework.

○ Find a TV program they like to watch (and maybe you don't like); have the child tell you about it. Or just watch it with them. Don't necessarily use this time to teach anything; instead just be more open with what they are doing.

○ Plan daddy-daughter and father-son outings with each child individually. Do something they choose, listen to what they want to listen to, and make yourself accessible to what they want to talk about. Be specific in your planning and do this activity soon. Be sure to record the results in your journal

○ Take some time to pray with just them. We often have family prayers as a group, but rarely do we think to be with our children as they are praying alone.

○ **A must**—sometime soon, go to your child's room and just stand there and watch him or her sleeping. Think about this child as a son or daughter of God and consider his or her potential. This is an amazing activity that will make you more accessible.

Responsibility

○ Being more responsible means that you could spend more time finding out about your children's friends. For example, make a lunch appointment or just visit with one of your children's friend's dads. Find out what that dad thinks of your child and learn more about the challenges he is feeling with his own son or daughter.

○ Meet with the local school principal and find out what is going on at your child's school. Schedule at least half an hour with him or her and explore the breadth of the challenges facing the kids at your child's school. How big of issues are sexting, drug use, truancy, vandalism, and so on? Be open to learning about the problems in your neighborhood. You may want to also find ways of becoming a helper in your child's school or with school events to get a better feel of what is going on.

O Meet with your children's church leaders and Young Men or Young Women leaders individually. In the same way as above, find out what the challenges are with the kids in your ward. Be open to suggestions from them about your children.

O If your child is going to an event in the next two weeks, find out more about the event. For example, find out who is going to be there, the nature of the event, and potential problems that could be found there.

Becoming "Intentional"

I began this chapter by saying that fathering is more about raising children than cows. I have been asking for you to consider in depth what it means for a father to "Preside, Provide, and Protect."[18] I think most of us get the "provide" part of this equation, but I wonder if we really know what it means to preside and protect in today's crazy world. To help answer that question, I believe that the "more than cows" idea can be condensed in a single word: intentional.[19]

The word "intentional" indicates that something is done with purpose: the opposite of intentional is accidental. Accidental parenting is invented on the fly. It is family home evening lessons that are made up as you go. On the other hand, intentional Heartbeat fathering is anticipating a child's needs and preparing for them instead of just responding to a needs once it happens.

We frequently hear the maxim from President David O. McKay: "No success in life can compensate for failure in the home." I am wondering how much we really put that notion into action. Too often family life and parenting is compartmentalized and put on hold until we get home from our "real" job in life—making a living. Of course, I am not suggesting a smart father quits his job and becomes a full-time, in-home parent. However, a smart dad will want to make sure he is putting the needs of his children high on his list of priorities.

This chapter has asked you to consider your ideology and motivations for what it means to be a father. The point has also been made that an intentional and thoughtful father considers increasing his father involvement significantly.

Remember that our core ideology is the motor that powers the rest of the car: Elder Dallin H. Oaks said, "What we see around us depends on what we seek in life."[20] As we begin to see the role of father differently, and begin to more fully embrace the idea of becoming intentional, our children will flourish in wonderful ways.

PFI: What Is a Dad?

In this interview, explore with your children what they think the role of a father is. Of course, you have to be ready for this interview. It may well be that you won't get the kinds of responses you dream of. It is very important to not defend the kind of father you think you are. It is also effective to not keep fishing for compliments with an expectation that you want them to vote you "father of the year." Just listen. Hear what they have to say. Here are some suggestions for getting started.

1. As usual, begin several days before the interview thinking and writing ideas down. Have you heard your children make comments about other dads they know? How about your father? Do they know their grandfather well and what his parenting style is (was) like?

2. Refer back to the notes you took about your own commitment to be an involved father.

3. After the opening prayer and after you have taken time to explore the events that are important to your child, ask something like the following: When you think about the fathers you know, tell me about dads that get along well with their children. What is it they do to be a good dad? When you grow up, what kind of dad do you want to be? (If your teen is a girl, ask her what kind of dad she would like to have for her children).

4. Finally, ask them what the best times are they have with you.

5. As you close, be prepared to tell them a short, two-minute story about your dad. This will take some thought. It should be a story

about how your dad was a strength to you. Even if this assignment is hard, follow through. It is important for your children to hear you "bear your testimony" about your own father. Again, I realize for some that will be a challenge. If you don't have a good story to tell about your own dad, think of a dad you know that you could tell a story about.

6. Make sure you record what happens, your feelings, and your thoughts following this assignment.

Virtue #2: Know the Needs of Others

Heartbeat Dads Take the Pulse of Their Children's World

No man on his death bed ever looked up into the eyes of his family and friends and said, "I wish I'd spent more time at the office."
—*Author unknown*

I RECENTLY STUMBLED UPON A SERIES OF PICTURES OF POP-SINGER idol Lady Gaga. One of her outfits made the news and was on the front of *Vogue* magazine. In this picture she was shown in a "meat dress." Chances are your kids know a lot about Lady Gaga; do you? How much do you know about her life? Are your children listening to her songs? They probably have heard them—they have likely downloaded them or cross-loaded them from a friend. Let's do a little quiz about this current pop icon.

1. Can you name any hit songs by Lady Gaga?

2. Do you know anything about the lyrics of her songs?

3. What do you know about her fall 2010 appearance at the MTV Video Music Awards?

You can find the answers to the quiz on the Internet. It should take you about five minutes. For questions one and two, take a look at the words to her hit song, "Born this Way." For question number three, type in "Lady Gaga VMAs" and read about her appearance. You could also type in "Lady Gaga meat suit."

Recent Big Changes in Culture

I grew up in the 1960s and, like many baby-boomers, thought our generation would also be the coolest. But am now finding myself way out of touch with current American youth culture. Do you feel a bit like that? The world of Lady Gaga and many other media-based phenomena are about two solar systems removed from the world I grew up in. Maybe it's only one solar system from your world if you grew up in the 1970s or 1980s. If you were a teen later than 1985 or so, you are probably more familiar with and "get" the world of Lady Gaga and associates.

The romanticized ideal of the 1950s and early 1960s is captured in this cartoon—things have changed.

The above cartoon captures a sentiment about fatherhood in the 1950s and early 1960s. It is a romanticized ideal that existed primarily in the imagination of the public. Fathers were the noble breadwinner, mothers worked only at home with their children, and everyone was quite happy and pleased with their roles and responsibilities.

Today's parents face issues and problems that were not even thought of fifteen years ago.

When I was a preteen, a big parenting concern was children sitting too close to the TV; they were worried about TV giving off radiation (a big topic when I was a kid). Parents rarely talked about the amount of time we spent watching TV or even about its content. Prior to the 1980s, most families got four stations, ABC, CBS, NBC, and PBS (PBS wasn't a factor until the 1970s). In the 1960s and '70s, TV was new, exciting, and relatively harmless compared to the barrage of uncensored material that seems to abound on what a friend of mine calls "today's hundreds of channels of nothing."

In November of 2011, the TV program 20/20 ran a special entitled "Too Young to Be Sexy?" In this provocative episode, the newscaster said the following about six- and seven-year-old girls, "We are really eroticizing childhood in ways that are harmful because it is showing girls that the only way you should be dressing is in this very sexy outfit." [21] The show's producers went on to show very young girls being taught how to be sexy and sexually appealing as pre-ten-year-olds.

By contrast, in my small rural town in the 1960s, parents were concerned with whether or not girls should wear pants to school. The length of skirts was a big deal also; I remember watching a friend get sent home from ninth grade English class because her skirt was too short and revealed her knees (I think the teacher made her kneel on the floor as the final, humiliating test). Imagine that happening today!

Most of you are probably not as ancient as me, but the principle remains. The world you grew up in, whether it be the '60s, '70s, '80s, or even the '90s is different than the 2010s. I frequently hear the claim that each generation of parents thinks the last generation was a "golden era" and this new generation is going to the dogs. I am not sure that is true—but I am sure that each new generation faces slightly different issues than the previous did.

For example, the current generation is struggling with something new called "sexting." I am a board member for the National Campaign to Prevent Teen and Unplanned Pregnancy. In a recent publication by this organization, [22] it was reported that about 20–25 percent of teens (ages 13–17) in a representative national survey had sent a text containing a personal seminude or nude photo. That number jumps to 35–40 percent for older teens. Let's face it, sexting wasn't a big issue when you were a kid—right?

The point is that Heartbeat dads need to understand what is happening in their children's world. You don't have to learn how to text at one hundred words per minute to be a smart dad; it is paramount to understand how these types of tech devices have changed our world. Some dads think the answer is to build a bigger castle with taller walls so they can hide their children from the influence of the world. I think those dads are barking up the wrong pile of stones.

There is no castle big enough or walls tall enough to barricade our children. Our world has changed dramatically with increased access to the Internet and the constant media barrage. Escape is impossible. We are in a situation now within which we are experiencing nearly universal contact with drug and gang cultures, music and music lyrics that would have shocked even the most liberal musicians and listeners of only a few years ago, and the emergence of alternative lifestyles that were only hinted at prior to the 1980s.

For example, my childhood TV viewing was really quite benign; in the beloved queen of all sitcoms, *I Love Lucy*, the lead character, even though visibly ready to give birth at any minute, was not allowed to use the word "pregnant" on the show.[23] In 1967, Ed Sullivan (of the Sunday night TV show *The Ed Sullivan Show*) demanded that the rock group *The Doors* replace lyrics from their hit song *Light My Fire*. He wouldn't allow the potential drug reference "girl, we couldn't get much higher." By contrast, today's song lyrics openly talk about vivid and explicit sex, the killing of police officers, and use and promotion of drug and alcohol use.

As a more humorous example, in my era, toilets were not allowed to be shown in movies or TV; the first reported viewing of a toilet was on an episode of *Leave It to Beaver*—however, the censors would not allow the toilet seat to actually be shown; only the top part of the tank is visible in the episode. Trends and changes in censorship have happened so rapidly that one pundit recently quipped that there are things on prime-time TV now that only a few years ago would have resulted in the local station owner being shut down. Prior to 1976, the television industry self-regulated it's prime-time shows. During this era, the industry established what was known as the "family viewing time" policy. That policy was overturned in November of 1976 by a federal court that deemed it a violation of free speech. Since that time, television producers and sponsors show what they think the public will tolerate. The trend has been for increased violence, crudeness, and sexuality.

It is not my intent here to spark a debate about the merits, pluses, or minuses of TV, texting, video games, or movie censorship. I am only suggesting that what our children see and hear in today's world is starkly different from what was allowed to be made public just a few years ago. And, I submit, you will simply be unable to keep your children from it if your only strategy is to build a bigger castle. Of course, I believe that protecting children from the world's influence is a key job of parents, especially fathers, but the notion that we can sequester children from culture seems to me to be an unattainable goal. We will spend more time on this topic later, but I would like you to start thinking about where you stand on this issue. Principle #8 captures the idea that one way to know what you should do about the rampant change in culture that you may find objectionable is to know the territory. You grew up in a different time and place than your children, and to better understand them, you should get to know their territory.

Principle #8: You Gotta Know the Territory

Your teen's world is different from your world. If you try to make your children live in the world you were comfortable with, you will be less effective.

Taking the pulse. A song from an old musical comes to mind. The musical is called *The Music Man,* and the song I am thinking of is called "Rock Island." The persistent refrain in the song comes from the salesman who is repeating the line, "you gotta know the territory." Knowing the territory of our current culture doesn't mean you have to jump in the pool and swim in it. The foundational virtues you adhere to haven't changed, but the point is that the times and topics have.

Before you assess the culture your child lives in, it is probably a good idea to think about the culture that dads now live in. In a recent book by Kay Hymowitz called *Manning Up, How the Rise of Women Has Turned Men into Boys*, the premise is simple. She reminds us that during the early 1970s and into the 1980s, when today's adults were children, American culture was in something of a "You Go Girl" mood. Women's rights and women's ideological goals collectively shifted. Additionally, today 57 percent of all college grads are women; women are making more than men at entry-level jobs throughout many of the larger cities and most industries. Our culture in general has shifted its view of the relevancy and even necessity of having men around.

We will soon pass a rather shocking demographic marker: for both black and white women living in the U.S., more than 40 percent of children born this year will be born to an unmarried mother.[24] That doesn't necessarily mean there is no man around—he may be there and even be committed to the relationship—but not obliged by marriage. A key problem facing today's dads is ambiguity. The fallout from the kinds of trends reported by Hymowitz and many others is that today's men are growing up in an ambiguous fog. One consequence is that young men today hesitate to even date with purpose; there is a serious trend of "hooking up" and being together with groups of friends as opposed to picking and dating someone with the idea of forming a permanent relationship. Consequently, men are unsure of their role as men, let alone as fathers.

As I said earlier, ambiguity leads to indecisiveness. Men tend to feel ineffective because as their children get older, they don't know how to adapt very well. Let's add this topic to the list of things that may be contributing to the ambiguity-fog. Men may feel stupid as fathers because of the fall-out from the cultural tectonic-plate shift we have been experiencing. That shift centers on both men's and women's relationship and role definitions undergoing serious redefinitions for about forty years.

For example, women (and American culture in general) are just not going to tolerate young men who promote the drill sergeant, macho, aggressive, and authoritarian fathering style. So young dads are unsure what they are supposed do or be in the fathering role. Add to that their uncertain feeling about their children getting older and more demanding and a perfect "family-crisis storm" is in the making.

The upcoming activity asks you to reflect on this storm as it relates to you. The reason it is important to reflect on this issue is that until you recognize the forces that may be shaping your attitudes and fears about being a father, you may not be able to increase your level of effectiveness.

JOURNAL OF THOUGHTS
The ambiguity fog and you

The purpose of this journal activity is to heighten your awareness of the sources from which you understand your role as father.

1. Rate yourself with regard to the following. The scale goes from 1 to 5. Give yourself a 1 if you feel very ambiguous about the item; rate yourself as a 5 if you have no ambiguity about being a father—that role is very clear to you. If you are somewhere in the middle, give yourself a score of 2, 3, or 4 to rate how ambiguous you feel about role as father.

Very Ambiguous   1   2   3   4   5   Not at All Ambiguous

Do you know what is expected of you as a father with regard to
_____ 1. helping your children with their homework?
_____ 2. being available when they are worried about friend relationships?
_____ 3. taking them to activities and appointments?
_____ 4. disciplining when something goes wrong?

2. Read the above section to two friends who are fathers. Have them rate themselves on the ambiguity scale as well. In a discussion with each friend, explore with them their greatest fears and dreams about being a father. Do they think the role of fathering or of men in general has changed during their lifetimes? If so, how?

3. Write below about this activity and what you found. Also, record how your findings might help you understand how to be better as a father.

_____
_____
_____
_____
_____
_____
_____

Activity: Know the Territory

The goal for this activity is to find out new things about the culture your kids live in that you didn't know about before. Then develop a FHE lesson about diversity. Work closely with your spouse as you design this lesson. Spend some time talking with her about how best to approach this topic. It is critical that both of you be on the same page about this lesson, why it is important, what the goals are, and what ideas should be left for another time.

Preparation: Begin this activity by listing what you do know or think you know about your children's likes and dislikes, fears and challenges.

What are your kids interested in?_____

_____

What kinds of music do they listen to? _____

_____

What are their favorite video games? _____

_____

Favorite movies? _____

_____

Favorite TV programs? _____

_____

Favorite books? _____

_____

Activity Caution: Chances are you don't know all the answers to these questions. Keep in mind that it is not your fault; most teens go to great lengths to be secretive. There is a difference between being deceitful and just being private. As kids gets older, they want to have parts of their world that are private. It is an expression of independence critical to becoming a young adult. So try to avoid getting offended if you find out you didn't know everything about them.

Strategy: Having a FHE about diversity in likes and dislikes will lead to greater tolerance and acceptance of family members. Build a family home evening around people's likes and dislikes. The principle to be taught focuses on tolerance and acceptance of what others value and like—things they might like that are within the family's range of acceptability. Like most of the FHE activities in this workshop, the activities tend to focus on older children, so you may have to adapt the lesson if there are younger children in your family. As I work with dads, one thing I have noticed is that often most FHE lessons target younger children and, therefore, the older children are bored to tears. Dads (the person who presides) need to figure that out and work closely with their partners on how to adapt lessons appropriately to different ages.

Knowing the territory of your children. While it is critical to learn more about the world you live in as a father, it is even more important to understand the cultural "pool" your children are being tempted to jump into. It is very possible that you don't know as much as you think you know about what they like, what they are watching, the pressures they face, and what they care about in our culture. Maybe you do know a lot about their world. If so, then I say hooray for you. That is something you should put into your journal as a success. But I often talk to dads who are quite out of touch with the video games, lyrics, music styles, and cultural heroes that capture their children's imaginations. They really don't know what their children believe in or what influences are shaping their lives.

Several benefits come from finding out about their territory and the pool they are being invited to swim in. You should become familiar with that world, its temptations, and its strengths. By knowing something about the culture your children face, you will know better how to respond. You will also have a better idea of how to compare the world they are being sold with what you believe are better ways of living life. You will find better ways of promoting the truths you want to convey in a way that speak to them. Your world is not their world (sounds like a scripture—do you remember Isaiah 55:8–9?). So find out about it. The activities above should help you in that first quest.

Scripture and church history examples. Consider finding and sharing examples in scripture or in current church leadership of people with different styles, likes, and dislikes (for example Moses versus Noah; Nephi versus Moroni; Joseph Smith versus Brigham Young; President Monson versus President Hinckley). Perhaps you have members of your ward bishopric who have different styles, likes and dislikes that could serve as examples. And, certainly, compare yourself to your spouse with regard to differences and similarities.

Tactic: Develop a short questionnaire. Take some time to develop a short questionnaire (maybe about fifteen questions total) that is designed as a quiz about what family members like and don't like. Notice that here and in all the activities that follow, I am only going to provide some directions to consider. I am not going to write the questions for you; you should be the one to mold these principles and ideas to your individual situation. Here are some examples to get you started:

What is the last book this person read?

What are this person's favorite kinds of movies?

If this person were banished to a desert island and could only bring one book, movie, or video game, what would it be?

What is the favorite musical group of this person?

How about world events? What do they know about what is happening in the world, or what world events are worrying them (if any)?

What do they think are the big issues at school? What are their peers getting in trouble for at school?

Lesson flow: Begin the lesson by explaining that we grow stronger together as a family when we know more about each other. The second idea in the lesson could be that diversity is a good thing. If everyone in your family had the same likes, dislikes, talents, and abilities, life would be boring. Try to get family members to realize that it is the mix of different kinds of people that makes the world a richer place. By contrast, you might also suggest that there are a few things that you hope the family shares that are similar to each other. Think of three or four important religious or other values you hold that you hope everyone shares and tell your family about those. (Hint: don't take more than about five minutes on this; it is not the point of the activity.)

Hand out your questionnaire and have family members fill it out. As a possible wrinkle to this activity, have the family members guess what others will say about you, your spouse, and other family members. The questionnaire could be a quiz to see if they know what each other likes.

Key. Use this FHE activity to generate a safe haven for talking about the culture.

Warning: Try at all costs to avoid condemning or evaluating the choices people are sharing. The point of this activity is to get people interested and sharing what they like. And, of course, by having them share, you will get an enriched insight into what they believe and—at least, hopefully—a little closer to knowing what they like.

Personal Father Interview: Lunch or dinner? As a follow-up to the FHE lesson, ask the child (or children) of interest to go out to lunch with you. Think through how to approach them about what they think of current music or media personalities, music trends, movies, and cultural events. Again, it is critical that the conversation not be about reforming them, but be more about getting to know what they like. Show interest—genuine interest is never forgotten. Interest that has an agenda attached will only be seen as manipulation.

Being intentional: Remember that fathers are more successful with their children when they are more intentional and invested. Use this activity to practice the idea of intentionality. It could be a theme for a whole month. Your prayers, thoughts, talks with your spouse, and chats with children could feature your interest in your children's world. Being intentional is not particularly easy. It takes time and investment, but it will pay off.

JOURNAL OF THOUGHTS
How well do you know the territory?

Be honest in your evaluation. That is, don't be overly critical or optimistic. By evaluating how things went, you can do a better job at future activities and at being a more effective dad in general. Here are a few questions to get you started.

How comfortable were you taking the lead in designing a family home evening? How did your spouse respond to you taking the lead? Is that the norm, or was it unusual?

_____

_____

_____

What are three or four new things you learned about yourself as you completed this activity?

_____

_____

_____

What are three or four new things you learned about your children? Be as specific as possible. What were the surprises?

_____

_____

_____

How is their world different from the world you grew up in? Discuss this last question with your spouse or a friend and take careful notes about the differences.

_____

_____

_____

_____

We Can Do Better—Without Going Crazy

As we get closer to our children and get to know their world, we can begin making modifications in how we parent. We can also commit to facing life's challenges. A Heartbeat father take the challenge and tries to change the way he looks at his child's world when he is trying to make a change for the better. One of the more important and difficult changes that has happened in recent years is the unhinging of dad's role with regard to how he interacts within his family. What is the image his children will have of him as a lead person in the group?

A key way our world has changed is in how we treat our children when they don't do what we want them to or when we are worried they might do something we don't like. In days gone by some authoritarian fathers ruled with an iron fist. Consider the following story from a friend of mine who was a child in the 1950s:

I'll tell you right now, there was no talking back to my dad. He was a very stern father—kind of a man's man. He worked in the local steel mill, and his father had worked there before him. When he came home from work, my mother would give him a list of infractions we had done during the day. Literally, each night we got a whippin' for something. Hardly remember a day when I didn't get the switch or belt. I never remember him coming to a school activity of mine or helping in the kitchen either. His world was working and giving us discipline. My mom's world was making food, cleaning house, and caring for children—those two worlds were as different as night and day.

For just about as long as anyone can remember, families were raised in an agrarian society. Life revolved around the farm. Men worked the fields, and women worked just as hard but usually inside the home. Their job differences were clear, and there probably wasn't much talk about changing who did what.

Children were taught obedience for a good reason. If someone left the gate open and the cows ruined the garden, it could be a life-or-death mistake. Punishment was often physical and had an escalating level of pain attached to it based on the seriousness of the offense. Everyone knew that it was the dad who was the law giver and the law-enforcer.

In today's world, there are few things a child could do that would warrant those types of authoritarian and physical responses that were so common just a few years ago. Back to our ambiguity premise for a minute, not only are children moving quickly through different stages that require different skills, and men's definition of who they are and their perceived relevance being brought into question, but in addition, men used to respond to family members in ways that have dramatically shifted in only one generation. Today's fathers are a first generation trial case in this regard. And, for the most part, these changes have been for the better. The bad news, however, is that these changes also come without mentors.

Today's generation is comprised of men whose fathers really don't understand the current cultural world of youth. Like the cartoon shown earlier, it is no longer enough to just be an economic provider and law giver. Today's fathers are expected to be a counselor, mentor, and interventionist with their children. The fathers of the last generation did very little of that kind of parenting. Therefore, today's fathers are having to do some inventing about how to effectively create the fathering role for this generation.

So if today's fathers are not only judged by how well they do the provider role or even by the measure of being an effective enforcer-dad, what are they supposed to be? I would suggest we explore an important principle here as a way for us get started on what it is we can do, given that the territory has changed so much.

The principle we use here is the War in Heaven Principle. As I get older, I realize I was totally blindsided with the idea that no matter what a parent tries (either here on earth or apparently in heaven) or how many times you pray, go to church, read books, or invest with all your heart, people (namely your children), at the end of the day, make their own choices.

Principle #9: The War in Heaven Principle

People get to choose. People, especially as they get older, get to make choices about their own lives. This life is their test, and we as parents can't make those choices for them!

71

Because I came from the older and less-informed generation, I expected children would do what I asked, become what I wanted them to become, and think what I thought they should think. Where have I heard that before? It seems like there is a story in the scriptures that covers that way of thinking. Doesn't it seem like if a dad tried really hard, tried to do all the right things and invoke all of the great principles he knew, his children would at least all grow up to be semi-famous, be married in the temple (the temple you have in mind would be even better), get their Eagle Scout and Young Women awards, have 3.2 wonderful, brilliant children themselves, live in appropriate-sized brick homes (with a nice guest room for grandparent visitors), and only have problems that involve calling a plumber? It turns out that we live in a new world where children ultimately get to make their own choices and do what they want!

Principle #9.1: You Can't Change Principle #9

You can't alter that principle, and if you
try it will only makes things worse.

Good parents sometimes get carried away trying to make their children into a copy of an ideal and, inadvertently, try to take away the child's right to choose. Some parents I know have what I would call the "desperate parenting syndrome" (sounds like a promising TV series, eh?). There is a ton of pressure on parents today (especially LDS parents) to make sure their children turn out a certain way and are able to not only crawl over the ever increasingly high "bar" but also leap over the bar like their shoes are filled with flubber (look it up—its an old Disney movie called *Son of Flubber*, or there was a 1997 remake simply called *Flubber*). The parents are stressed, the children get stressed, and the pressure to be high-performing as a parent or child is quite palpable. And unfortunately, the parents sometimes resort to an 1800s Puritan style of parenting and pull out a belt (either literally or figuratively) to try to make someone do something they don't want to do.

Okay then, what are we supposed to do? On the other hand, I also don't want to say to parents, "Don't worry—everything will be fine, lower the bar if you feel the pain." You are probably not ready to lower the bar anytime soon *and* you can't drag out the belt or the water board for just a little torture. A key point of this book is that there is another way. The principles in this book are a start in knowing what to do.

By employing the War in Heaven principle, we realize that life is about choice. So we, as parents, do the best we can with the best principles we know. We become invested and interested in our family's well-being and then realize that children will, inevitably, make choices that may give us some heartburn—or worse.

Chances are that if a dad gets a bad case of desperate parent syndrome, panics, and turns up the heat, demanding better performance at the cost of the relationship, he will only make things worse. Some DPS parents try to create prison compounds or become abusive drill sergeants; some create feudal castle systems within which they think they are the king (or queen) and mistakenly believe they are in total control. Our only hope is to realize that in our times, teenage children expect to be able to make choices at increasingly earlier ages. Our religion teaches the power of personal choices, as does the culture we live in. It turns out that our job is to guide those choices and not think our job is to make the choice for them.

Sometimes we think we just need to build a stronger castle.

In summary, your job is to work yourself out of a job. That is a key role of the parent. You are not tasked with having children and then charged with making their decisions and controlling their movements like the great puppet master. The following activity should help you get started on thinking this dilemma through. Again, intentionality means that the change and effort here has to begin with you.

Activity: FHE Lesson on the War in Heaven

○ Read the story of the confrontation between God, the Savior, and Lucifer in Moses 4. I would suggest you read this together with your spouse.

○ Next, reread the LDS Conference address offered by Elder Robert D. Hales in the 2010 October Conference entitled, "Agency: Essential to the Plan of Life."

○ Also, read the following conference address by Sharon G. Larsen given in an LDS Conference in October 1999. This talk is an excellent one for helping you and your partner think through what it means to provide direction and guidance to children without jumping into the war-in-heaven problem of forcing people to do what you think they should do—no matter what they want to do.

○ Once you have completed the readings above, develop a family home evening around the idea of what agency is and how family members can use this principle in their dealings with one another. The following are some suggestions. Note that these suggestions should be seen as starting points.

○ Read the quotation of C.S. Lewis in Sister Larsen's talk about temptation. Teaching children how to deal with temptation, as Sister Larsen explains, is a key to understanding how to build strong families. Getting a bigger club, giving more time being grounded, or adding more restrictions will only promote more push-back, resentment, and hostility.

○ Make sure your audience knows what agency is. The talk by Elder Hales should help here.

○ Consider using hymn #240, *Know This That Every Soul Is Free,* in your discussion. You may even want to have it as a theme for the week.

○ Your job as the dad in this lesson is to explain to your family that as their father, your responsibility is to teach them to act on faith, teach them to make good decisions, and then help them to live with the choices they make. Your harder job will be to show them that you can live this principle as well. Remember the Inner Working Model principle and that how you administer your family will be the model of how they believe God administers to them in their lives.

○ As you form this lesson, make sure you take careful notes about your feelings and thoughts. Prayerfully approach this task and be willing to begin the process of changing how you deal with your family members.

○ Once you have taken the above steps, read the following conference talk for more ideas and directions: Richard G. Scott, "The Plan for Happiness and Exaltation," *Ensign*, Oct. 1981.

Virtue #3: Gratitude
Heartbeat Dads Teach the Virtue of Gratitude

*Gratitude is not only the greatest of virtues,
but the parent of all the others.*
—*Marcus Tullius Cicero*

I watched Scott take the struggling child from the wheelchair. He soothed her struggling, flailing arms and gently laid her on the blanket and pillow in front of the TV. Jayne is twelve years old and for ten of those years has been fighting just to stay alive. She contracted a virus when she was a baby. The ensuing fever lasted for days and was devastating to her brain and her future development. Unable to walk, speak, or communicate, Jayne's only form of communication is random arm movement that tells when she is excited or distressed.

As he positioned her on the makeshift bed, Scott whispered to Jayne, "Tell Randy hello, Jayne." The ongoing monologue between Scott and Jayne is tender and revealing. "Do you wanna watch some football, Jayne?" Scott inquires. To the untrained eye there is no response from Jayne, but Scott knows she can hear. I say hi to Jayne. Scott and I talk.

He tells me he won't be able to come to the camera club meeting later in the week because it is his night for "poop duty" as the family calls it. Jayne goes to the bathroom infrequently, and two to three times a week, it is Scott's turn to give Jayne an enema and perform the physical therapy motions necessary to assist Jayne in a bowel movement. This is a lengthy process. As Scott jokes about being on poop-duty, my love for him and his family grows; I realize that what Scott is doing behind the scenes is heroic.

That afternoon, our conversation turned to gratitude. I wasn't surprised at all to hear Scott tell me of his deep love for Jayne, but his next comment caught me by surprise. He told me how grateful he is every day and night for the opportunity to serve Jayne and be her father. I have never known Scott to complain or brood over the fact that a random disease robbed his daughter of a typical childhood or that she will never play soccer, go on a date, or attend college. The virus and its results were a sad day for Scott and Rebecca, Jayne's mom. But today his heart is full of gratitude and love for this precious child. Scott told me,

It is sometimes hard for our family to take care of Jayne, but overall the blessings to our family have been enormous, and I am truly grateful for this opportunity. This challenge has changed our family." He then explained, *"The biggest blessing is of compassion. Our other kids love Jayne and know what it is like to serve a special needs child. I believe having Jayne in our home has made our family stronger.*

Scott and Jayne having some time together.

I have been around Scott for many years; I have watched him work with and for his family. The challenges with Jayne could have had a variety of effects on Scott's family, but Scott took a leadership role and chose to turn this tragedy into a family strength. One of the tools he found was in how he defined what Jayne meant to his family. His family knows that Scott thinks of Jayne as a blessing for which he is thankful everyday. There is no doubt that his children know what is in Scott's heart when it comes to Jayne.

He chose to view Jayne's problems in the ways that reflect a sense of gratitude; he didn't have to choose that response. He could have cursed God. He could have blamed his wife. He could have decided to emotionally divorce himself from the situation and become immersed in his school and work. There are many choices Scott didn't make. I admire Scott for the heroic choice he made to man-up and lead his family in times of anguish. His leadership is founded on the premise of gratitude instead of platitudes. He chose thankfulness instead of distance and shame. He chose to be a man among men instead of whining about what could have been.

In the next few pages, we are going to elaborate on that theme. Learning to be a person of gratitude is the first step in being able to teach gratitude to your teen. I used the words "learn to be a person of gratitude" deliberately. My experience is that most of us, especially men, are more likely to view the world in terms of what could have been and what needs to be done instead of how things are and how magnificent life is. This chapter is built on the notion that becoming a man with a thankful heart helps strengthen your family and allows you to then teach this virtue to your children.

In the first section, I introduced the heartbeat metaphor. This chapter extends that idea and suggests that an effective father not only is a constant influence (like a heartbeat) but recognizes that the blood that flows through the veins is common but precious. We infrequently think about the essential nature of blood—without it we would die within a few, short minutes. Men and women of virtue are more likely to take note of the common routines of daily life, the unique qualities of their teenager, and the routine joys of being together with family. In short, this chapter is not about an extravagant show of thanks. It isn't about the huge fiftieth anniversary party during which the husband says, "Thanks." Instead, fathers who build strong relationships with their spouses and their teenage children know how to frequently acknowledge, recognize, celebrate, identify, and cherish the ordinary flow of love each day.

Overall, this book is about several key virtues effective fathers use to strengthen families; gratitude is the mother of all other virtues. In fact, the level of gratitude in one's soul and in one's family is a moral barometer. Emotions of thankfulness and actions of gratitude are true indicators of how we see relationships. When a person or family scores low on the thankful/gratitude barometer, they are also much more likely to score low on relationship quality and strength.

In addition, the research reported below tells the story about how gratitude is an inhibitor of trouble in a person's life. People with higher levels of gratitude for others are much less likely to act in ways that damage relationships. Having a grateful heart is a first and vital step in building what researchers call "pro-social" behaviors. Pro-social behaviors are actions toward others that consider the needs of another over their own needs. When we collectively act in pro-social ways, families run smoother, businesses do better, and the tasks of life are easier. When gratitude is lower, pro-social behaviors are less likely to occur and family members make choices based on self-interest rather than thinking of the group.

> ## Principle #10: Gratitude Is the Parent of All Virtues
> As family members focus on the valuable gifts each person brings to the family, it is harder to make decisions based on self-interest.

One of the key points of the above principle is that we often forget that virtues like gratitude have a purpose and function. Gratitude works. It is not just a nice thing to do because someone told us to try it. Sure, obedience to God's laws is important, but they are laws because they work—they aren't just arbitrary. In this section, I am suggesting that you try to increase the levels of gratitude so that you will be a better leader in solving family problems, administering tasks, and initiating meaningful family activities. Of course, the correlate to that idea is that you can't teach gratitude unless you are living that principle. This is one of the clearly marked areas of life wherein if you try to teach something you are not living, the "hypocrisy detector" will scream like a city tornado warning.

To be clear, gratitude isn't just about being polite and saying thank you to the wait staff at a restaurant; being a person with a thankful heart is much more. It is the reflection of what you really think and believe about those around you—both those you know and understand and those you don't understand. The highly critical and dismissive person has a hard time finding anything to be thankful for when he is around people he doesn't like or agree with. On the other hand, a person who has learned to be a person of virtue and has a grateful heart looks for the good.

I am also suggesting that fathers should take a strong leadership role in teaching teens how to have more gratitude for all of life's blessings. Of course it is a good message from either mothers or fathers, but it seems to me that when children see their father humbly giving thanks to God and those around him for all that comes his way, the impact will have a slightly different effect than if they only see it from one parent, especially when that parent is the mother. I have no research to back up this claim, but I think women are more likely to promote gratefulness in children than are men.

Some men may, I hypothesize, see teaching virtues like gratitude as "women's work." Therefore, if that is true, showing your teen how gratitude works in your world (work, church, family, and play) will be an important elaboration for them. Of course, we are entering an age where many mothers work outside the home, so teaching children about how these virtues work in non-home settings from as many perspectives as possible is an important strategy.

There are several activities at the end of this chapter to help. However, if you are like me, you will need to boost your own gratitude score before you try to teach it to others. Spend a few days or even a week or more on this chapter. Experiment with looking for positive attributes in those you are in contact with. Begin by experimenting with the Your Gratitude Score activity (forthcoming) by yourself. Keeping a daily gratitude journal for even two weeks can be a powerful intervention. As you try that activity yourself, you will then be in a much better position to teach the virtue of gratitude during a family home evening or in some other informal setting.

What Is Gratitude?

Gratitude is a sense of thankfulness and even an attitude of joy about the gifts we receive. There are many kinds of gifts we might receive; some come from friends, some are unexpected, some we probably don't deserve, some come from family and we do expect them, and some come from nature and from God.

The word "gratitude" comes from the Latin word *gratia*, which has at its roots in the idea of grace and a sense of appreciating and acknowledging all that is great or wonderful. According to one author, the core ideas behind this term are the words "kindness" and "generosity," and acknowledging when we receive something from another.[25] Having a grateful state of mind not only is highly prized in our culture but has been seen as the core of other virtues since antiquity. Indeed, Judaism, Christianity, Islam, Buddhism, and Hinduism all hold that gratitude is an essential characteristic of the truly spiritual and virtuous person. In fact, the religious texts of the world and many philosophical theologians are very clear that an ungrateful heart may be among the most egregious of sins.

Only Aristotle seems to have had a different view. He believed gratitude was a sign of weakness.[26] He wrote that the truly virtuous people were self-sufficient and it was demeaning and humiliating to take anything from another. He believed the core of most virtues was what we would call self-sufficiency. Being grateful, therefore, was a sign you had received something from another and you were diminished as a virtuous person. This is an important point to contemplate. You may want to ask yourself if you are more Aristotelian in your thinking—do you believe that a core virtue of the virtuous man (or woman) is self-reliance and self-sufficiency, or do you believe that the most virtuous person is one who recognizes that what he has and who he is is more of a gift from God, family, and community? Don't try to dodge your answer by saying it is both. Of course, there are elements of both in most of us. But, overall, are you a person whose life is primarily centered on self-sufficiency, or a person who feels connected to others and feels that your success in life is a reflection of the grace and help from others? One way some may think about this philosophical dilemma is to focus on our thanks to God. Some, I believe, are thankful to God that He has blessed them, but they then believe that who they have become in life is primarily because they have willed it to be so.

The scriptures can help us think through this problem. Many scriptures speak of the power of gratitude. Read these thoughts again, and ponder what they mean to you. I have inserted a couple of my thoughts after each scripture:

"And in nothing doth man offend God, or against none is his wrath kindled, save those who confess not his hand in all things, and obey not his commandments" (D&C 59: 21). This scripture asks us to make sure we recognize God in all things, including being thankful to your own parents for giving you life and raising you.

"That ye contend no more against the Holy Ghost, but that ye receive it, and take upon you the name of Christ; that ye humble yourselves even to the dust, and worship God, in whatsoever place ye may be in, in spirit and in truth; and that ye live in thanksgiving daily, for the many mercies and blessings which he doth bestow upon you" (Alma 34: 38). This scripture touches a bit more on being thankful daily for all we have, but it only focuses on directing our thanks to God.

Elder James E. Talmage said, "Gratitude is twin sister to humility; pride is a foe to both."[27]

Here is part of a talk by Marion G. Romney from an LDS general conference in 1980:

> While we have made great strides in the (welfare) program since that day, the principle still applies. Everything we do in welfare services must be measured by its accomplishment in spiritual terms. Givers must give out of a righteous heart and with a willing spirit. Receivers must receive with thankfulness and gladness of heart. The Spirit must confirm a bishop's evaluation regarding assistance. It must lead a home teacher and a visiting teacher to know how to respond to needs of families to whom they are assigned.

President Thomas S. Monson said in conference, "My brothers and sisters, to express gratitude is gracious and honorable, to enact gratitude is generous and noble, but to live with gratitude ever in our hearts is to touch heaven."[28]

The quotes above focus on two types of giving and receiving; of course, the first is a focus on giving thanks to God. Certainly, that is a key element for the virtuous dad to attend to. However, there is another aspect. Expressed gratitude (action instead of words) is also a foundational cornerstone of living a virtuous life. This is particularly true in family relationships. Remember the first principle I shared with you in the book, the As I Have Loved You Principle: this idea reminds us that our relationships with others will be enhanced if we model how God loves us. Learning to be a person filled with gratitude and being willing to teach children how to be grateful are brilliant examples of that principle. At the same time, we should also teach that doing as much as we can for our own well-being is a critical and important principle as well.

When we fail to teach teens to be grateful to God, their parents, other family members, and their communities, they will be handicapped as they reach for their potential. Again, teaching thankfulness and gratitude is more than teaching children to be polite.

The story in the Book of Luke[29] about the ten lepers moves us a little closer to the idea of thinking about gratitude in ways that are not just having a thankful heart to God. The lepers all cried with one voice to the Master, "Heal us and have mercy on us." But when they were healed, only one returned to offer thanks. And the scripture says he was a Samaritan. Remember that they were thought to be of a much lower social class than the Jews in the region. The Jews hated the Samaritans, and the Samaritans hated the Jews. So this story of a hated person that gave thanks when others didn't would have caused some raised eyebrows at the very least. The story of the lepers is a pillar of Christian theology and has been for two thousand years. For me, this story teaches us to be ever mindful of those who help us and those who share our path in any way. The following JOT asks you to think about the idea of self-reliance versus recognizing others' influences in your life.

JOURNAL OF THOUGHTS
Thanking God or being thankful
to God and community?

The Aristotelian notion is that gratitude is something of a weakness. Aristotle believed that self-sufficiency was a core virtue. Most religions of the world teach that we live in a world where self-sufficiency is important but that who we are and how we get along in the world is a gift from God *and* from a host of others we meet on the paths of life. What are your thoughts about this difference? Here are some questions to consider:

Do you see yourself as a person of self-sufficiency? Is this like you or not like you at all?

_____

_____

_____

Perhaps you are a person that is *very* thankful to God for all the gifts He has bestowed upon you. But do you believe that the rest has been up to you? Or maybe in your heart-of-hearts you believe that who you are and what you have achieved is mostly something you have done on your own with God as a distant observer?

_____

_____

_____

Are you a person who is deeply thankful to God *and* to those around you who share your path of life? In other words, you see clearly how your life is loaded with gifts from God, gifts from others, and without those gifts no amount of hard work would have mattered?

_____

_____

How Do Researchers Measure Gratitude and What Have They Found?

Social scientists have been examining the role of gratitude in relationships seriously for about twenty years at the most. There is not a large stack of studies done about gratitude because most of us in the family science arena usually study what is going wrong with families. It has been, historically, quite difficult to get something published about the positive elements of family life and even more difficult to write about key virtues like gratitude. But recently, that trend shifted. In 2002, a team of researchers[30] started asking a serious research question: would people do better in life if they had a more appreciative and thankful outlook? They started their research with the individual (not families) and found that individuals who were more grateful and appreciated those around them remembered both pleasant and unpleasant life events better than did those who were less thankful.

These researchers and a few others followed this research line and began studying other effects of using gratefulness as a strategy. In one often-reported study[31] it was found that people who recorded grateful thoughts in a journal were more likely to feel better about their lives and reported fewer physical aliments during the period of the study. In a follow-up study, they also found that when young adults recorded daily thoughts of gratitude in a journal, these participants were far more likely to be alert in school, have increased enthusiasm for life, and report more determination and energy than did a control group who only wrote down each day what their day was like.

In another study, it was found that young adults who wrote in their gratitude diaries daily were also significantly more likely to reach out during the day and provide help to someone who needed support with a personal problem. The opposite effect was recorded when another similar group was given the task of recording the daily irritations and hassles they encountered. The later group was nowhere near as helpful and supportive as the group who recorded feelings of gratitude. If you read these studies carefully, there is no reason to assume that one group was somehow different than the other in the beginning. It really does seem that writing down daily thoughts of gratitude makes a world of difference in one's outlook.

Those who only focused on the hassles of life consequently attended to complaints, the drizzle of life, and all that was going wrong.

In our study of emerging teenagers in the Flourishing Families Project, we wanted to know more about children's gratitude, and we tried to find out if there were there certain types of parents who promoted more gratefulness in their children. Here are the questions we asked five hundred teens in our project.[32]

Activity: Your Gratitude Score

Respond to the following questions using a 5-point scale of 1 (very much unlike you) to 5 (very much like you).

Very Much Unlike You 1 2 3 4 5 Very Much Like You

_____ I have so much in life to be thankful for.

_____ If I had to list everything that I felt grateful for, it would be a very long list.

_____ When I look at the world, I don't see much to be grateful for.

_____ I am grateful to a wide variety of people.

_____ A great deal of time can go by before I feel grateful to something or someone.

_____ I always express my thanks to people who care for me.

_____ I often feel grateful to my parents and family.

_____ I find myself complaining about life frequently.

Record your score here:

Once you've done the next activity and had your teen take the same survey, record your teen's score here:

(You may find it interesting to guess what your teen will say. Or, instead of guessing what you think they will say, record how you think they really do see this issue. In our research, we also compare the responses of both parents. You may want to consider doing that as well.)

Activity: Your Teen's Gratitude Score

1. Have your teenager take the same survey. Try to do it in a way so that you are not looking over their shoulder. If you can't get them to take the survey or you think they wouldn't answer the questions honestly because they know their parents would look at them, it is okay to use your guesses about what they would say as a substitute. In the Flourishing Families Project, we asked teens to rate themselves and to have their parents rate their gratitude. It turns out that the scores from the parents and the scores from the kids were nearly the same. And, that was true for our LDS sample as well as the non-LDS sample in Seattle. The only person's score who was a bit off was the mother's score. When mothers rate their daughters' level of gratitude, it is significantly higher than the father's rating of her or the teen's rating of herself.

2. Once you have rated yourself and your teen (either as a self-assessment or based on your rating of him or her) do some observing over the next week or so. Assuming you have access to your child, during a week's time, how many times did you hear them voice thanks or gratitude? Jot down on the chart below your results for each day.

	Number of times heard thanks	Comments
Day 1		
Day 2		
Day 3		
Day 4		
Day 5		
Day 6		
Day 7		

3. Our research shows that fathers rate their daughters at about a 3.6 on gratitude and they rate their sons lower at 3.3. Moms rate their daughters about a tenth of a point higher but rate their sons about the same level of gratitude as do the fathers. Kids' view of themselves in our sample of five hundred teens about the same as the parent's view except the daughters rated themselves lower than did moms and about the same as the dad's ratings.

4. Comment here on your findings. Were you surprised? What did you learn about yourself? How does your score compare to the research study? If there is a difference, what do you make of that?

_____

_____

_____

_____

_____

_____

_____

5. With the above data in hand plan a PFI with you child. The details of the PFI are found in the next activity. Make sure you try and avoid turning this PFI into a lecture session about gratitude. Also, be very careful about presenting data. By that I mean I recommend you don't lay the above chart on the table and show the child how they did each day. If a teen believes you are spying on them every day and taking notes about what they say, it will probably decrease the level of trust they feel toward you.

PFI: Gratitude

1. Find a quiet place and time. Turn off all phones, TV, music, and so on.

2. Begin with prayer.

3. Small talk is essential. Find out how his or her week has been.

4. Prepare a two minute thought about gratitude and share that with you teen. Include in your two minute thought a short of list of things you are thankful for. You should mention that you have noticed several times when they were thankful—based on the first part of this activity. Be specific in what you have seen.

5. Suggest that you would like to try something together with them. Explain that several researchers have found that it helps us have a greater sense of direction in life when we look for things to grateful about.

6. Prepare in advance to have two small notepads ready for this assignment—something they could put in their back pocket or in a small purse. On each of twenty pages, write consecutive dates starting with the current date. Make it so that each new day is on a new page. The directions could sound something like, "Would you try an experiment with me? I read about an experiment during which people were asked to simply write down things they were thankful for each day. They were asked to record any specific thing they were thankful for." You may want to provide the numbering on each page, one through five.

7. Explain that you would like to have you and your teen record at least five things they are thankful for each day for three weeks. I would recommend here that you demonstrate this by pulling out your small journal and writing down your five items for today. Share those with your child. They should be specific things that reflect what has been happening to you today. For example, you could be thankful for getting to work on time, having a warm bed, getting an e-mail from a friend, or the friendship of your spouse (can you be specific about something she did today to remind you that she is your friend?).

8. Ask if they would be willing to try the experiment. If they don't want to, don't force the issue. But tell them to jot down ideas about thanks as they think of it. The worse thing to do would be to turn this into a power struggle. You won't succeed at this activity if someone feels forced to do it. Make sure your child knows that you are doing it together and that at the end of three weeks you want to meet again and share your results. Schedule a date to meet again and compare notes.

9. Conclude by sharing with your child three or four things you are thankful for and include at least one item that mention them. As I mentioned in the introduction of this book, these kinds of activities work better if you adapt them so that they come from

your heart. In other words, avoid using this book in a visible and open way. I recommend you don't say something like, "It says here in this book that we are supposed to do this dumb activity." Instead, just do the activity and make it feel as much as possible like it comes from you. I am not asking you to be dishonest, instead I am asking you to take the core of this idea and make it yours. If you do that, your success will be much greater than if your child thinks you are only doing this because some book told you to.

Ordinary Savoring: Stop and Smell the Popcorn

Savoring at Bryce Canyon, Utah

In 2007, Bryant and Smart[33] wrote a book that caught my eye. These researchers introduced the idea of savoring as an extension to the notion of gratitude. Savoring means to appreciate fully or to relish. When we savor an experience or moment, we are fully engaged in that moment. We drink it in without distraction. Savoring also implies that we are fully involved—not just as an observer but as a fully vested actor in a situation.

Take a look at the picture on the previous page. I'm sorry it is in black and white, but you can get the idea.

When I visited Bryce Canyon, I found it quite overwhelming in scope. It was almost too much to absorb. Its beauty and grandeur were overwhelming. I took several pictures like the one you see above. That day the sun was shinning on the red rocks, making wonderful shadows and light trails. It wasn't until much later that I really started looking at the pictures more closely. While I was there, I'm sure I was in tourist mode and not really seeing or savoring—mostly I remembered being overwhelmed. However, as I began looking closely at this picture, I noticed a tree. Do you see it on the right side, about a third of the way up on the top of the cliff? I realized that that tree was much larger than one in our yard. Only then did I start to grasp the enormity of the canyon I was looking at.

Savoring a moment instead of "touristing" the moment means that we become, for just a few minutes even, fully engaged. We begin to see things we haven't seen before. We hear laughter in a different way, and sometimes we can unwind our tense muscles and let the music we are hearing drift into our souls. We aren't thinking about the annoying crying child in the parking lot, we forget the travel schedule, and we drink in the moment with full force.

Many of us have to take pictures of such scenes and then go home and ponder the scope and beauty of the moment later. I have taken hundreds of people to Europe on study abroad adventures and have noticed this too often. I am thinking of a time when we were riding a ski-chair lift to the top of a spectacular mountain near Lucerne, Switzerland. I was having a savoring moment that was intense. I can still conjure up that ten to fifteen minutes with amazing clarity and recall. I hear the huge cow bells on the Swiss cows as they grazed below. I hear the quiet hum of the cable moving over the pulley system as we gently rose up the slope, and I can feel the cool mountain air. The scene before us was dazzling: off to the right was the majestic Eiger mountain, and to the other side was the Jungfrau. When we got to the top, one of the students just behind me turned to another and commented how irritated she was. She wanted to stay below and look in the shop selling cuckoo clocks. She had missed the whole experience.

That is kind of sad, isn't it? But I am afraid we do the same thing in daily family life. I know this principle, and I find myself missing so much of the richness, humor, texture, and grandeur of family life because I am on my way to the next meeting or trying to find the car keys. The following principle encapsulates the idea that becoming a person who knows about "capturing the moment" can fill us with more thankfulness.

The reason I am including the idea of savoring is that I have come to believe that being a truly thankful and grateful person requires an ounce or two of savoring in the mix. I don't think we can fully be appreciative of our children or their needs unless we are drinking in the moments we have with them. For example, the point of playing a game of Monopoly with your family is not always to declare a winner. You may, in fact, use such times to just savor being with them and enjoy the moment regardless of the outcome.

Activity: Savoring the Moment

Here are some suggestions for building more savoring moments that will increase your level of gratitude for your children and spouse.[34]

1. Decide in advance that you want to experiment with savoring an experience. As I have mentioned before, it is critical that you not announce to the group that, "Okay, everyone. I am practicing my savoring right now. Could you give some space while I cherish this moment?" That isn't going to go well. Instead, privately plan a time when you know there will be a short time together with your teen or with your family all together.

2. While in that moment pay full attention. Engage in the experience as much as possible. Have all cell phones and external devices like iPads, MP3 players, TVs, and home phones on hold.

3. Try to note everything about the experience. What are the sounds of the someone moving their game piece around the board? Take careful note of the tone in each player's voice. Carefully pay attention to the laughter and the small talk.

4. Who is not talking? Who is more excited about winning and who is just playing for fun? How are people sitting? What are they wearing?

5. Don't overdo savoring. It doesn't work well to completely zone out and become a 'savor-zombie.' People will be referring you to mental health services. It only takes three to four minutes of careful, indepth, fully-involved savoring to capture a moment. In fact, when you try this, you will probably find that the image that is created in your brain, will stay with you far longer than a typical memory.

I recommend you find a way to teach this skill to your teen. In some informal setting that is planned but not over-structured, just sit with your child and relish the moment. Maybe you are together on a walk. Stop for a minute and have them close their eyes and just listen. Then direct your senses to the smells and the breeze. Chances are they will think you have lost all your marbles, but try to find a way to help them relish the simple moments. Folks that know how to attend to the world around them and savor the beauty of life are much more likely to find the good in the other parts of their world. Conversely, if you are only teaching your child to pay attention to the tasks, errands, responsibilities, and lists of life, they will probably miss an entire spectrum of color that builds a rainbow.

In sum, it is important to be a grateful father and teach that concept to your children. I believe that becoming a father who focuses on thankfulness is a key life skill and that gratitude is the mother of all other virtues.

We also explored the idea of savoring as a skill that can help you stop and really drink in the events around you. Once you drink those in and really "hear the music," you will probably find it much easier to be grateful and thankful for that moment, those people, that particular piece of prelude music being played, the laughter of that child, and the smell of the popcorn.

Virtue #4: Forgiveness
Heartbeat Fathers Are Forgiving and Teach Their Children the Art of Forgiveness

Forgiveness is a virtue of the brave.
—Indira Gandhi

David Clay decided it was time to check AJ's cell phone. Checking and monitoring AJ's computer and phone were a part of his weekly routine. AJ really didn't know it was a weekly routine but he did know that, on occasion, his personal life, including Facebook, email, and phone messages, were being checked. He was usually pretty careful about what went out or came in to the devices connected with home.

When David first saw the picture of Julie Black—in her underwear—laughing and flirting at the picture taker, he had a complete melt down. He didn't even know this girl. When had AJ been to a party? He could see other kids in the background; he thought he knew at least one of them. Why did AJ have a picture of this girl on his phone? He immediately thought of all the hours and time he and his wife had spent protecting AJ from this very thing. David also began rehearsing his fears about being a good parent. His anger toward AJ was increasing with every minute. David would eventually need to cope with his anger, and think through all of the facts of what had happened, including many facts he wasn't aware of in the first few hours. Then he would need to prayerfully seek to find a way to cancel the debt.

When someone trespasses on our property or family rules, or we feel they have wronged us, there is an interpersonal debt that is incurred. This story is not about how David and Pam should punish AJ or whether they should take all cell phones away. Nor is it about the evils of pornography and the increasing levels of sexting that is happening in schools. Instead, this section is about how being a more forgiving father will build stronger relationship when things don't go the way you want them to and you feel like a child trespasses.

The dictionary tells us that to "trespass" is more than just hunting for deer on someone's land without permission. The word comes from Middle-English and Anglo-French, and it implies that someone has overstepped the bounds. A trespass is an uninvited infringement. When children infringe on family rules and step on the toes of family beliefs, we may respond with anger, hurt, fear, resentment, and regret.

We will return to the story of The Cell Phone Incident later. This case study will give us some insights about how one father uses the principle of daily forgiveness well, while another one doesn't quite get the big picture with regard to being a forgiving dad. The point here is that becoming a more forgiving father on a daily basis is a vital element of becoming a loving father. As I am sure you are aware, becoming a forgiving person is a demanding assignment; the natural guy in all of us isn't very forgiving.

Forgiveness is a sacred idea. The concept of forgiveness shows up in every major religion. It is prominently talked about in the Old Testament, and it is, of course, one of the key pillars of the New Testament. It is also a major theme of the Book of Mormon, Doctrine and Covenants, and numerous conference talks. It is a central message of religion. The following scripture is as about as clear of a scripture as it gets:

> Wherefore, I say unto you, that ye ought to forgive one another; for he that forgiveth not his brother his trespasses standeth condemned before the Lord; for there remaineth in him the greater sin.
> I, the Lord, will forgive whom I will forgive, but of you it is required to forgive all men. (D&C 64:9-10)

There is one part of this scripture I find jarring, "he that forgiveth not his brother his trespasses standeth condemned before the Lord." Most scriptures talk about results after this life. Or they talk about principles in general terms. However, this scripture is talking about the present. It says that our attitude about forgiveness is directly connected to our standing with the Lord—that idea gets my attention every time I read it.

In addition, I believe having a hard and unforgiving heart toward a family member magnifies this principle. Since forgiveness is the ultimate form of love, when we withhold our forgiveness (especially to family members) it is a damning and condemning statement about how we listen to the Savior's advice to love everyone.

More than thirty years ago, Elder Marion D. Hanks gave a conference talk[35] about this idea.

> The withholding of love is the negation of the spirit of Christ, the proof that we never knew him, that for us he lived in vain. It means that he suggested nothing in all our thoughts, that he inspired nothing in all our lives, that we were not once near enough to him to be seized with the spell of his compassion for the world.

He goes on to ask,

> What is our response when we are offended, misunderstood, unfairly or unkindly treated, or sinned against, made an offender for a word, falsely accused, passed over, hurt by those we love, our offerings rejected? Do we resent, become bitter, hold a grudge? Or do we resolve the problem if we can, forgive, and rid ourselves of the burden? The nature of our response to such situations may well determine the nature and quality of our lives, here and eternally.

Recent view on forgiveness. In 1984,[36] a book was published entitled *Forgive and Forget: Healing the Hurts We Don't Deserve*. This scholarly text prompted researchers to take a close look at forgiveness from a scientific view. Until that time, the topic of forgiveness was relegated to Sunday sermons and a few self-help books. Since then, there has been an explosion of high quality research about forgiveness and even a handbook on forgiveness.[37]

The take home message of this research is that when we forgive others their trespasses, especially family members, we do better and our relationships soar. So the scientific community and the scriptures agree: becoming a forgiving father makes good things happen.

JOURNAL OF THOUGHTS
What is forgiveness?

What is forgiveness? How do you define it?

_____

_____

_____

_____

Forgiveness is when . . .

_____

_____

_____

_____

What does forgiveness mean to you personally?

_____

_____

_____

_____

_____

_____

_____

_____

Canceling the debt. Susanne Denham and her research colleagues[38] say that forgiveness has three parts: emotional, thinking, and an action feature. She states that forgiveness is a method of *canceling the debt*. But before we can cancel the debt in full, there are several steps that have to happen first.

The first part of this process is that we recognize that we feel harmed; for example, when David Clay saw the picture of Julie Black on AJ's phone, he felt betrayed and hurt. His first thoughts were about disloyalty. And because it was disloyalty from a family member, the pain was magnified ten times. He thought he knew his son and what he was up to. David was certainly not ready to cancel this debt on this issue anytime soon. In fact, he was now on the warpath. And he was going to make sure this didn't happen again.

But forgiveness is not just a thought-game and we simply say—"ooh, sorry, I forgive you." Real forgiveness is a kind of makeover that happens. Here are some steps in the forgiveness makeover that help the process work better:

Someone harms us. This is the transgression step.

We feel emotions like fear, hurt, betrayal, anger, or contempt.

We gather information to find out what really happened while we try to put the emotions on hold.

We rethink the harm and try to understand the case from the other person's point of view.

We change our behavior toward that person: we talk with him, hug him, and tell him we are sorry about the incident.

Principle #11: Canceling the Debt

Forgiveness is the process of canceling the debt we think someone else owes us. The goal is to move on and let the incident become part of the distant past within which we learn from the experience without ruminating about details.

Forgiveness works! Research tells us that being a forgiving person helps us heal.[39] When we become more forgiving, our physical and mental health shoots up, and some studies even show that being more forgiving helps us live longer.[40]

Couples who know how to forgive are happier, have more stable marriages, and report more marital adjustment. Studies have even found that forgiveness decreases family conflict and aggression, increases communication quality, and creates an absence of relational aggression. Researchers have recently found that forgiveness is a key gauge of overall family well-being.

Forgiving Is a Process

Transgressions. The following is a list of a few wrongdoings families face:

A child steals something from a parent

Your teen tells you a lie; for example, a teenager is failing at school but conceals her failures through a web of elaborate lies.

Teenager tries smoking when she knows it is against family and religious teachings.

You find out your child has been cheating on homework.

You discover that your child has been tagging. ("Tagging" is the current lingo for painting elaborate graffiti on buildings, fences, and train cars.)

You find out your child has been terrorizing a younger sibling when you are not around.

You find out a child is bullying others at church and school.

You find out your child has been sent a sexting message.

You find that a teen has been accessing porn-sites on the family computer.

The following picture is of a scared dad. I watched this group only for a few minutes; here is what happened: This episode happened in a large metropolitan city during a special event. There were crowds of people everywhere. The dad told his girls to stay put while he bought the tickets; they didn't stay put. They started running and playing. One attraction led them to another. The dad came out—no girls. He immediately panicked. He started looking for them everywhere, his voice got higher and louder. Another onlooker pointed him in the direction where he had last seen the girls, and within a few minutes, I saw the father and his girls coming back toward the entrance. He was holding both their hands, walking pretty fast, and looked quite agitated. He took them to a secluded spot and let them know how angry he was with them.

This dad was scared—and it made him angry.

What happened next was powerful. Once he had laid down the law and had given them a good scolding, he hugged them in a persuasive show of affection and forgiveness. They got the message—actually three messages. First: "When I say stay put, I mean stay put; the world is a dangerous place." Second: the message was delivered, the emotion drained, and he saw how they could have been distracted and what they were up to. Third: he physically forgave them by giving a loving hug. There didn't seem to be any leftover anger. They left for the event and all was well. No one was laughing and giggling right away, but the anger and fear part were over.

The list of possible transgressions above is, of course, incomplete. For example, I did not include felonies, a child running away, or incidence of substance abuse. It is true that the forgiveness process is similar for those types of offenses, but I have chosen not to dwell on those bigger transgressions here. Instead, I want to stick to the ordinary wrongdoings. If we talked here about the larger felony-type of problems and drug use or examples of forgiveness about a drunk-driver killing family members, it would be too easy for us to gloss over the daily use of this process. But by focusing on the ordinary wrongdoings, the process will be more applicable to everyone. If you have had some larger more dramatic problem happen in your family, the principles we explore will work for those as well. My examples, however, are focused on daily life.

The following is a list of problems that came from 180 LDS parents in the Flourishing Families Project. When we visited them in their homes, we asked them what types of conflict and problems they dealt with during the last week before the interview. The following is a list of the kinds of problems they reported:

Lying

Breaking family rules

Bullying a sibling or other child

Doing something at school that gets the child in trouble

Breaking a Gospel-related commandment

Being disrespectful to parents and other adults

Sexual misconduct including dating, sexting, petting, and hooking up against parent wishes

As we work with the data from Flourishing Families Project, it has been interesting to note that few other researchers have thought to ask parents about the forgiveness that happens (or doesn't happen) between parents and children. Most of the research about forgiveness is about couples. Most of the stories you hear about forgiveness are about the drunk driver incidences, high profile murders, and other headline stories. Thinking about how a parent becomes a forgiving person is an unusual topic, but one that needs serious attention. As I observe parents and listen to colleagues who are counselors, it seems obvious to us that how parents respond to their children's transgressions is a critical aspect of how successful we are as parents. In particular, harsh and unforgiving fathers, in my experience, do enormous damage to their children's well-being and their family's stability.

JOURNAL OF THOUGHTS
Transgressions—name a few

When was the last time a child stepped on the toes of your family rules and beliefs?

_____

_____

_____

_____

List a few transgressions that have occurred in your family during the last year. As you read through the upcomimg material, think of these issues and try to apply the process and ideas to these specific incidences.

_____

_____

_____

_____

_____

How does your experience match up with other parents? List several events that have occurred over the last year for which you needed to employ the principle of forgiveness.

_____

_____

_____

_____

_____

_____

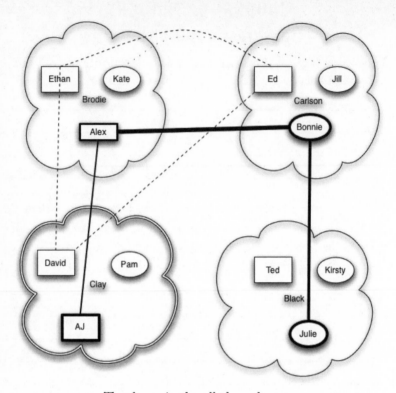

The players in the cell phone drama

Back to the cell phone incident. Let's return to the Clay family and the cell phone sexting incident. The primary character in this story is Alex Brodie.[41] We will get back to David, Pam, and AJ Clay in a minute. Unbeknownst to David Clay, the story of the picture of Julie on his son's cell-phone began long before AJ had anything to do with it. The above diagram will help you keep track of all the players in this drama.

Alex is AJ's best friend; he is sixteen years old, of medium height and weight, fairly good looking, and has about five good friends. Alex plays football every fall. His parents are Ethan and Kate. As the rest of the story unfolds, you may want to refer to the picture above to help keep track of the players in this teen melodrama.

Alex likes Bonnie Carlson very much and has a major crush on her (notice the bold line between her and Alex in the diagram). She is fifteen and a cute girl with a broad and welcoming smile (although right now her smile sparkles with braces). Alex and Bonnie have become an "item" at school, and Alex's friends are envious of the close relationship that is emerging between them. AJ is one of those friends who is the most jealous. He has a serious crush on Bonnie as well; Alex is the only one who knows that. Alex, AJ, and Bonnie all sit together during Mutual and have lunch together almost every day at school. And they text constantly.

Recently, Bonnie and Alex made some mistakes: as a joke, Bonnie decided to take a picture of her best friend Julie Black while Julie was getting undressed at a sleepover. She used her cell phone to take the picture and also to send the picture to Alex. The picture showed Julie in her underwear, but you could tell from the picture that it was clearly Julie. Sending such a picture is, in today's parlance, called sexting.[42] Alex also thought it was funny—because Julie was stepping into her pants and starting to tip over and fall into some pizza. He also knew the picture would drive AJ crazy because AJ was crazy about Bonnie. Alex found this whole love triangle very amusing and decided to tease AJ by sending him Julie's picture. Bonnie had no idea that AJ likes her a lot.

AJ's parents regularly do spot checks on AJ's phone. The spot checks were not something AJ was aware of: he believed his phone was private property. AJ's parents believed they had the right and responsibility to check up on AJ secretly to see what AJ was up to.

To make our story just a bit more complicated, it turns out that Bonnie's father (Ed Carlson) and Ethan Brodie (Alex's father) are in the same elders quorum at church (see the dotted lines in the diagram). Ed and Ethan are both friends with AJ's dad, David Clay; they know him through a mutual business acquaintance. Bonnie's mother, Jill Carlson, and Alex's mother, Kate, are also (of course) in the same ward but not close friends. The other two families do not know AJ's mother, Pam Clay. Julie lives a few miles away and she and her family are not members of the LDS church. Kristy and Ted Black are loving parents who don't permit Julie to have boyfriends at her age and are very careful about TV and Internet consumption.

So, that is the basic introduction to the wrongdoing and a brief overview of the players in this potentially explosive drama that is about to unfold. When the Clays found the picture of Julie, the resulting blowup impacted all four families.

The responses. David Clay was surprised and devastated. He had heard of sexting but didn't believe it was a problem with the kids in his immediate world and certainly not with a child of theirs. He instantly worried that AJ could be looking at pornography on the Internet; he also wondered about AJ's friend selection and what other trouble AJ and his friends could be getting into.

The first night after the Clays found the picture of Julie was difficult. David and Pam spent most of the evening talking about what to do—the long session included tears and praying. The Clays had carefully built an extra "wall" of security around their home. Their extra wall included Internet blocking services, no computers in children's rooms, limited cable TV, and careful monitoring of their children's media and video game usage, TV watching, and friend selection (notice in the diagram there are two walls around their family). They were shocked that this type of thing could have happened to them.

Late that night, the Clays asked if they could come over the Brodies' house and have a private chat with both Ethan and Kate. At that meeting, Pam and David showed the Brodies the picture and explained how upset they were by event. They further explained that they didn't know who the young girl was, but they were very disappointed in Alex's behavior and were clear that AJ would not be allowed to have Alex as a friend from now on. David and Pam explained that they were sure Alex was the one who had taken the photo since it had come from his texting address and signature, and they didn't want boys like Alex in AJ's life.

The Brodies were speechless. They assured the Clays that there must be some misunderstanding. Alex was not that type of young man—they knew him better than that and were sure the whole situation could be cleared up. The Clays were not convinced and indicated that they thought the Brodies were naïve about the situation and not taking it seriously enough. The Brodies didn't appreciate that tone, and the Clays left with the two families a bit confrontational with each other.

The next day, Ethan and Kate sat down with Alex and told him about the visit from the David and Pam Clay. They asked him about the picture of Julie that had been sent to AJ. Alex flushed: he was cut to the core and his face turned fire-engine red. He explained that it was all a joke and no harm was meant. He revealed that AJ had a secret crush on Bonnie and that he was doing it to tease AJ.

Ethan explained to Alex that AJ's parents were very clear he wasn't to be AJ's friend anymore and he wasn't welcome at AJ's house. Alex was truly upset and sorry. They had family prayer that night, and the hugs afterward were very heartfelt.

After family prayer, Alex and his parents continued talking about the incident and together they started to get to the bottom of the story. Reluctantly, Alex revealed that Bonnie had sent the picture. Kate and Ethan retreated to their bedroom to plan further what to do.

Kate decided that she would give Bonnie's mother, Jill, a call and set up an appointment to meet with her. During that meeting Kate and Jill had a long heart-to-heart talk within which they realized Bonnie had made a mistake and that it had to be dealt with.

Later Jill and Ed decided that Bonnie would have to surrender her phone for two weeks. They also decided to plan an in-depth meeting with Bonnie that Ed would take charge of. He thought that it would be better if he tackled this as a one-on-one with Bonnie so she wouldn't feel they were ganging up on her. Bonnie was distraught: with the incident made relatively public, she could barely even think about going to school or to church and facing her friends.

At the Clay residence, things didn't go well. Upon their return from the Brodie residence, David and Pam went to AJ's room. Since the Clay's don't allow doors on the rooms of their teens (a precaution to prevent secret unwanted behavior), they marched in unannounced and began a long and confrontational battle with AJ about his phone, sexting, and the quality of his friends. He tried, without success, to explain that he had nothing to do with the picture—it just came to him on the phone, and he had seen it but didn't even know the girl.

The result was that AJ's phone was confiscated, and he was grounded for four weeks, starting that night. He would not be going to the big school dance and party at the end of the week nor would he be allowed to go on the young men's activity camping over the spring break.

There is much more to this story, as you can imagine. The sexting incident had repercussions between all of the parents involved. Julie was horrified that a picture of her had been sent to Alex and her friendship with Bonnie was never the same after. Alex and AJ were both upset about the forced loss of their friendship—Alex developed a strong disliking for AJ's father, who, from then on, would not even make eye contact with him at church.

In addition, there was also measurable chill each time Ethan, David, and Ed saw each other socially or at work. Eventually, this incident became a watershed episode that ended up in the bishop's office, within which there harsh things said by all involved; the bishop tried his best to keep these families from hating each other. There was also spillover into the ward. The incident caused a great deal of angst and stress among the youth of the ward. It was a big deal for each of them, and Alex's reputation in the ward was damaged.

I could use up this whole book to talk about the fallout and issues that arose from this one careless act and the ways parents and leaders responded. However, for our purposes here, let's use the bare bones of this story to think about the power of forgiveness and, in particular, how a skilled father can use the power of forgiveness to help solve issues of transgression.

The "Affect" Element of Forgiveness

According to researchers, forgivingness has three parts:[43] the feeling or emotional aspect, the thinking part, and when we change our behavior toward the offender. Let's start at the beginning with the first thing that usually happens after a wrongdoing: emotions and feelings usually spray us down like an untended fire hose gone crazy. When AJ's dad first saw the picture of Julie on AJ's phone, he experienced a flood of emotions that left him wringing wet with guilt, fear, and a sense of failure as a parent. We have all experienced this tsunami of feelings that include fear, anger, guilt, anxiety, shame, regret, resentfulness, denial, worry, and self-pity. Of course, the more egregious the transgression, the more likely we are to experience a downpour of intense emotions. Since both David and Pam defined this event as very serious, they experienced an immediate deluge of emotions that left them trembling, weak, and barely unable to speak to one another. That they were able to put their emotional flooding aside long enough to visit the Brodies was actually remarkable. In fact, neither Pam nor David could sleep for the next two nights; they were fraught with waves of panic and even nausea from the extreme emotional flooding they both experienced.

Attributions. A key to this part of the forgiveness process is understanding the idea of *attribution and definition*. Immediately Pam began asking what this incident meant. She also began the "attributional" process. That is, she was instantly trying to assign causes and reasons for the occurrence. She was thinking, "Why did this happen when we have been so careful?" In other words, she was searching for the reason. She needed desperately to assign blame or causes to someone or something—hopefully not herself. Unfortunately, David and Pam both skipped any cool-headed investigation. Instead they jumped to judgment far too quickly before they had all the information. *Boom*—David saw the picture and attributed the problem to a defect in his parenting. Pam immediately blamed herself and then jumped to secretly blaming her husband, and finally her son. Instead of carefully unpacking the episode and finding out all of the details, the flood of emotions and her need to sooth those feelings resulted in a rush to judgment and punishments. In like manner, David wanted closure, retribution, and guarantees it would never happen again, and he wanted them now.

When we take this type of shortcut in relational responses, we are almost always bound to miss the important parts of the problem *and* we are much less likely to be forgiving. It is hard to be forgiving in a state of emotional flooding, and it is hard to forgive when you don't have all the information.

The first application message is that being able to forgive is easier when we *slow down*. When we are hurt, threatened, challenged, angered, and provoked by our children a key skill is to **not overreact**. Step back from the hurt; let the flood of anger, resentment, guilt, remorse, and fear subside. Then we can start considering all angles of the problem. *The rush to judgment will almost always cause stress and judgments that are unjust.*

Because David and Pam didn't collect good information about the event in a calm and careful way, they were forced to hang the sin on anyone or anything close by—including themselves as parents and on AJ. In doing so, they invited the **Shoulda-Woulda-Coulda (Mr. SWC)** monster to the relationship table.

Pam's first reaction was to blame and attribute the cause of this problem to herself, to her husband, to AJ, and to AJ's friend. By doing so, they quickly knocked on the door of Mr. SWC. She first and foremost blamed herself and started thinking of her own perceived failings as a parent: with light-speed she invoked a barrage of self-blame and flagellation. She started thinking of all the things she should have done, could have done, or would have done if she had only been a better parent.

By midnight of the first evening, she was sobbing uncontrollably and commenting on her failure as a parent and even said to David that this was further evidence that she should have never been a mother and how disappointed she knew God was with her. She continued to sob, telling David that he should have taken more care to protect AJ and they should have built a better barrier between the outside world and her children. All of the shoulda-woulda-couldas she could think of came pouring out in one long sobbing session.

The next target in her grief was David. It didn't get fully explored in the first night, but it would in the next few days. She clearly attached some of the problem to him: she just knew that if he were taking a stronger leadership role in the process that these kinds of things wouldn't be happening.

I call this type of over reaction *horribilizing*. Horribilizing is when we jump to conclusions long before we have carefully gathered data and taken the time to find out what really happened. We respond only to the emotional element of the wrongdoing, see it as rather one-dimensional—it was right or wrong, and then blast off with accusations and responses that are often way out of line and rarely fit the crime.

Turning it around using the attributional approach. A better way to respond could be found at the Brodie household. Ethan Brodie did feel some of the same emotions that were tearing the Clay house apart, but he knew things would only get worse if he let those monsters direct his thoughts. He backed off from blaming, quick attributions, and horribilizing. Instead, he was able to reach down deep and look at the picture from a more *benign point of view*.

The benign approach. The term benign, for our purposes, is best understood by thinking about its opposite—malignant. Think of a malignant cancerous tumor. A benign tumor is a problem but it doesn't contain the deadly explosives that a malignant one does. Ask yourself this question—honestly. When a child or spouse does

something you don't like, do you automatically use this as evidence
to prove your case that

this person is a jerk;

this is another example of how she is a disobedient brat;

this is another instance of how this person has failed me;

this is another case where you never do what I want you to do?

The above responses are examples of malignant attributional
thinking. You are assuming that whatever the person says or does is
another example of how stupid or disobedient they are. Now tie that
thought to forgiveness—it doesn't work does it? Bringing the malignant assumption to the table means you are nowhere close to having a
heart that is predisposed to forgiveness. Instead, when we think this
way, our heart becomes hard and we think of the person as disobedient, period. We probably then continue with the thought that unless
they are willing to change, you are unwilling to give them any slack.

True, it may be that at the end of the day you will find out that
the child was, in fact, disobedient. The difference is that malignant
attributional thinking means your first thoughts are that this child
is an out-of-control brat and this is yet another example of that fact.
Our thinking in this case doesn't really have very much to do with
the actual incident—but instead it is about affirming our belief that
this kid is a brat.

Bringing the benign attributional assumption to a situation
means that you are prepping yourself for forgiveness. Let's use a
very common example to show the contrast between malignant and
benign thinking. Case: child spills milk at the table. Responses: The
malignant way of thinking produces responses like, "Bernice, this is
another example of your disobedience. I have told you ten thousand
times to put your milk in a place where you aren't going to knock it
over." The benign way of thinking does not necessarily assume that
the act was an example of disobedience. Instead, your first thought
is "children at this age are sometimes clumsy. I know we have gone
through this before, but it was an accident."

Back to the sexting example. Truthfully, from my observation,
AJ wasn't trying to break commandments, wanting to engage in sex,
willfully breaking family rules, thinking of hurting someone, nor
were they a signal he was interested in pornography, nor did this

event mean he was even experimenting with sexting. In fact, this was the first phone message he had ever received of this nature; and he was at a complete loss about how to even think about the event. His parents were right to be concerned, but they probably overreacted by horribilizing about what they thought it all meant. Their heavy dose of malignant attributional thinking and self-flagellation by the mother contributed to a response by the parents that wasn't very helpful.

David's immediate and energized negative attributions about how he thought about this event framed much of the sequence that followed. Further, once he had gone down that path, he found it difficult to invoke the forgiveness process at all.

Most of us will go to great lengths to protect our responses when we feel violated, even when we know our responses are completely indefensible (you might want to take a peek in your scriptures at this point about the destructive power of unbridled pride).

Therefore, our second principle has to do with attributions. This principle basically says that we are better able to forgive others when we are careful with the emotional/attributional element of a perceived transgression.

Principle #12: Attributions in Forgiveness

Be careful about attributions. Make sure you consider as many possible reasons for a perceived transgression as possible. Try to develop the skill of thinking in terms of the benign assumption rather than immediately horribilizing and embracing a malignant assumption when something goes wrong.

The application of this idea is fairly simple. We will be much more able to deal with the emotions of these situations if we first seek to understand the full story and consider a range of attributions or possible reasons why someone may be doing something. Most of us are not very good detectives. We jump to conclusions and don't slow the process down when we feel we have been wronged.

The Thinking Element

The best way to approach a wrongdoing is to first calm the emotions and then think through the event with a strong emphasis on discovering the details. Try to uncover as much evidence as you can; leave no stone unturned. Reserve judgment. Before we get to the place where we can forgive, we have to be calm and allow the Spirit in. Wouldn't you say that it is very difficult for the Spirit to be with someone who is angry, hateful, animated, and overemotional? Job "one" is to keep our emotional part of the brain from completely hosing down the whole situation with adrenaline and cortisol. These type of hormones keep our pulse rate high, and they invoke very primitive feelings of wanting to fight or flee.

By contrast, when we suppress our fear and anger, we are much more likely to listen to all sides of the issue as dispassionately as possible. This calmness and repose helps us make better judgments.

The picture above is from a World War II poster used in Britain during the Battle of Britain. During this time, there was an advertising campaign that encouraged people to not overreact to the bombing and threat of invasion. This poster is a favorite of mine and works well as a reminder to parents. Keeping calm and allowing your thinking self to do its job is a key to successful parenting.

Ledgering. One way that dads sometimes use their thinking self in a negative way is when they employ *ledgering*. This notion has been around for several decades in the counseling literature. When someone trespasses and steps on our interpersonal toes, the emotional punch leaves us wanting to perpetually remember the egregious event. We feel the need to remember so we won't get stung again. It can be a protective measure. Or we remember so we can accurately trounce the person in the conversation about their faults and wrongdoing the next time as a kind of revenge tactic. Being the best ledgering person in a fight helps us remember the necessary details of past transgressions and that gives us the competitive upper hand.

The following are words of the father of Ron Goldman. In 1994, Ron Goldman was a waiter at an LA restaurant called the Mezzaluna Trattoria. Nicole Simpson had apparently left her glasses in a case at the restaurant, and Ron agreed to drop them by her house. He was unlucky. He somehow stumbled into the Nicole Simpson murder scene and was also brutally murdered. While O.J. Simpson was found not guilty in the murders, Ronald's father never relented in his passion for bringing O.J. to justice. In 2007, Ron's father, Fred, finally obtained the rights to a never-published book, *If I Did It*. In an article published in the Washington Post in 2007,[44] the following was written:

Goldman has never let the most notorious murder case in modern American history, the O.J. Simpson trial, move "more than a centimeter from the surface of the brain," and today he launches a bizarre offensive against Simpson, the man whom a civil court—and many Americans—consider to be someone who got away with murder. "To let it go would be tantamount to saying, 'It doesn't matter anymore,' " Goldman says of his continued pursuit of O.J. Simpson. "I made a promise to Ron," Goldman says in a long, late-afternoon interview in his modest home, "that I would pursue this [jerk]. That we would never let this go."

The unforgiving person "never lets this go." To protect ourselves, or to soothe our consciences, to seek revenge in attempts to make things right, or to remain in control of others, we build elaborate ledgers of all the crimes, wrongdoings, hurts, and the results of the criminals actions and then we don't let them go.

These ledgering systems are like the long-lasting gobstoppers in the movie *Willie Wonka and the Chocolate Factory.* The ledger-holder remembers every mistake, dollar wasted, error made, and can give you details about what you were wearing and the time of day when the crime was committed. In short, they *ruminate* about all transgressions, wrongdoings, misdemeanors, sins, and offenses great and small ever perpetrated against them.

Rumination. What a great word to describe this destructive process. If you recall from your biology class, cows have four stomachs. They eat their grass or hay, swallow it, and it partially is digested by a bacterial action. Then they cough up their semi-digested lunch (cud) and chew it again—sweet, eh? This process of further breaking the plant material down into something they can use is called—ta-da—rumination (after the name of their stomachs). That is what an unforgiving person does.

The unforgiving person spends a significant part of their waking life coughing up the cud of yesterday's transgressions and rehashing, rethinking, re-chewing, reconsidering, reexamining, reassessing, and reviewing every detail and aspect of what happened, what they said, what she said, what you wished you would have said (or not said), and even how to get revenge.

Principle #13: Rumination and Ledgering Make Forgiveness Difficult

A key step in forgiveness is learning to do less ledgering and ruminating about past sins, transgressions, and wrongdoings. An important step in the forgiveness process is developing the ability to make thoughtful judgments about a problem and then let it go. This type of healthy response promotes forgivingness.

Have you ever eaten a bad piece of steak and the more you chewed it, the bigger it seem to get until you felt like you were going to gag on it? Each time we rehash, rethink, re-chew, and regurgitate the old story of how our child didn't do what we thought he should, the story expands; it seems to gain new life. We chew harder and longer getting angrier and angrier. Ruminate, ruminate, ruminate—at the heart of re-chewing our transgression cuds are the roots of relationship destruction. The emotions remain and the event becomes a mythological centerpiece of how we feel about that person.

Turning the rumination around. A key step in becoming a more forgiving person is to learn how to suppress the rumination. This is not easy. These reoccurring thought patterns are like tire ruts in the frozen snow. When we are prompted in any way to remember a certain topic or person, our wheels crunch into the frozen ruts, and it is as if we can't steer free.

In extreme cases, such as post-traumatic stress syndrome, a pungent odor, loud car door slamming, or the smell of a certain meal cooking can trigger an *uninvited memory* to start replaying. These uninvited memories seem to have a life of their own. This happened to David and Pam, for days following the sexting event; they both found themselves, as they described it, "deep in thought." What they meant by that was that any mention of AJ, cell phones, the Brodies, or even of church, triggered a flood of new emotions followed by a "video replay" of the event and what was said.

That was followed by another set of emotions and reenactments within which Pam, especially, recounted to herself what a rotten parent she was and how worried she was that AJ was going down the road to ruin. Those frozen tire-rut thoughts would inevitably lead to speeches in her head she wanted to give to David about how he should be a better father.

One way to interrupt the powerful frozen tire-rut thoughts is through thought interruption and replacement. The minute you feel the tire crunching into the frozen rut, force yourself to replace the thought pattern with something else. Grab your scriptures and read something uplifting and wonderful in them—I try to avoid, in these situations, scriptures about judgment, numerous sins, and all the things I should be doing better. Instead, there are plenty of scriptures about people of courage such as Ammon and David, stories of awe like the nativity story, the travels of Paul, and scriptures about the intricacies of the gospel, like the oath and covenant of the priesthood.

I also like to read books about history events (the life of John Adams, for example) or even some novels and movies can help dislodge my thoughts. However, be careful in your thought replacement attempts. Some movies and novels make the situation worse if the message of the movie is dark and fraught with interpersonal struggle.

Psychologists also tell us that increasing our physical exercise is a good way to fight the frozen tire-rut syndrome. As you are walking or biking, try listening to inspiring and soothing music rather than hate-talk radio or other types of music that stimulates negative or aggressive thoughts.

Just for a minute, try this experiment. Switch your thoughts momentarily to the sounds around you that you may not have heard before. Do you now hear the clock ticking or the soft sound of the furnace-forced air flowing into the room? Perhaps you hear a car go by that you weren't paying attention to.

The mind is a wonderful thing. But in reality, it thinks in a straight line. It can really only consider one thing at a time. You can make it switch back and forth very rapidly, but, in fact, there is no such thing as multi-tasking. That is why talking on cell phones and texting while driving is so dangerous. We have the illusion that we can monitor what is going on in front of us and talk and pay attention to the phone conversation at the same time. Actually, we are switching back and forth like a manic TV channel flipper looking for a good station.

The point is we can change our focus. We don't have to allow a thought pattern to run its course. But it does take practice and discipline.

Next, try prayerfully asking for help. This is a simple but effective strategy also. These are exactly the kinds of prayers that can and are often answered. God could but probably won't reboot your mind so the frozen tire-rut is not there, but He can and will prompt the worthy petitioner with ideas about how you can help yourself. Be sure to try the suggestions you think of when you pray for help.

My last suggestion for thought interruption is service. If a child (or anyone for that matter) offends you in some way, find a way to immediately get closer to that child by doing something for him or with him. The Savior says to us in our sins and in times of need, "Come unto me"; He doesn't push us away and tell us to come unto Him later when He feels better about us.

Dads also need to be accessible *especially* when things are rough. Go to the child, make eye contact, ask about their day, offer to help with a problem, and offer a soft touch. Several pieces of research have shown that simply touching the arm of the person you are talking with makes a powerful and lasting positive connection.

In our sexting story, one of the huge differences between David Clay and Ethan Brodie was this exact skill. When relationships were rocky, David became even more conflict-avoidant than he usually was. Deep down in his soul, he was terrified of having to face confrontation. So he would retreat and became distant, moody, interpersonally cool, and unapproachable.

Ethan, on the other hand, knew that when things got difficult the best thing to do was to strengthen the connections with his son instead of retreating. Within a short time, it was Ethan's leadership that actually strengthened the connection Alex had with his parents. Ethan employed the benign assumption principle, got the full information about the incident, didn't overreact, and turned the situation into an effective teaching moment. During that teaching time together, Ethan listened with intent—making eye contact and kept his attention focused. He frequently touched his son's arm and reassured him. At the same time, he wasn't sending a parenting message that reeked of permissiveness, but he used the situation to reinforce family and gospel principles and the seriousness of sexual purity. His leadership in this situation made all the difference in the outcomes.

Changing Our Motivations and Behaviors

Some researchers suggest that saying "I forgive you" is probably in most instances an indication that one is ready to start the process. The problem for most of us is that we think saying "I forgive you" is the whole thing, and then we just want to move on!

However, actions are almost always more powerful than these types of shallow pronouncements. So let's talk about how to get to the next step by changing our behavior toward the wrongdoer. I have already indicated that one way to interrupt the frozen tire-rut thinking is to do something for that person, serve them, speak to them, acknowledge them, and hug them. That is the beginning.

If we don't change our behaviors toward them, even if we are still healing ourselves, then we run the risk of letting the anger and resentment grow within us. The behavior change by us is a much stronger statement about how we really feel. Words are cheap. Behaviors are worth much more in this equation of healing. The overt act of reaching out helps the person really know we still love them despite the problem.

Finding ways of changing our behavior by first praying for offenders. A key scripture tells us one way we can begin to really understand and even embrace those who transgress against us. In Mathew 5:44 the Savior says, "Pray for them that despitefully use you, and persecute you." That has always been difficult for me and maybe for you as well.

I suggest that one of the most important behavioral changes you need to make is to find out what to do next by praying in very specific ways when trouble occurs. Of course, it is a wise thing to pray for them at other times as well. But, when a transgression occurs, praying for ideas about what to do next is a key strategy for becoming an effective dad.

Explore with the Lord the motivations of the child, the reasons why things have happened, and what to do next. Ask specifically for some ideas of what to try next. Being specific in prayer requires some thought in advance. Try the following:

PFI: Learning about Forgiveness and Sharing It

Find about thirty to forty minutes for this exercise.

1. During the first ten minutes or so, read several passages from the scriptures about forgiveness. There are plenty to choose from and can be found in the topical guide in your scriptures.

2. For five minutes think of the offender without thinking of the offense. Force yourself to think of them in another context. See them laughing at the basketball game. Imagine them playing in the yard with a sibling; remember the day they were born or the day they were blessed.

3. For three minutes, shift your thoughts to the problem and briefly

write down in bullet points the flow of events. For example, in our sexting example, one would write down the information about the picture, the response from AJ's parents, the possible lying, and so on.

4. Now, take this scenario to the Lord with specific questions. And remember there are some petitions that are probably inappropriate—like, "Lord, I can't do this. Please turn back the clock and let me have a mulligan on this one." Or, "Lord, make AJ's mother go away. She is such a bad parent and I need a way to tell her how poorly she is handling this situation. How should I do that?" Instead, a better prayer might be, "Lord, I am struggling knowing how to help Alex talk to Bonnie about why sending this picture of Julie was inappropriate. I love both of these children and I have such high respect for Bonnie's family; but I need some ideas about how to approach Alex effectively so this incident won't drive a wedge between us."

5. Now for at least five minutes, sit and re-ponder the situation while thinking of the child—not in wrongdoing—but with a smile on his or her face. During this time, listen for strokes of ideas. Earlier I quoted Joseph Smith's counsel to listen to "strokes of ideas."

6. Next, jot down your impressions, thoughts, and ideas. As you keep a journal, consider keeping a journal about these kinds of thoughts rather than a diary of daily events. These kinds of ideas are the gems of life and shouldn't be forgotten.

7. It is time to act. Take the ideas you have gleaned from this exercise and do it. Don't wait and don't hesitate. Make it so. Warning: if you ask the Lord for help, and you receive strokes of ideas about what to do, but then you ignore or shrink from the task, the likelihood of getting good ideas in the future is probably going to be reduced.

8. Find the appropriate way to share your thoughts on forgiveness with your child. You may want to use the experience from above.

9. As you share the results of this activity—as much as is

appropriate—find out from your children if they are having trouble forgiving someone. With the ideas and knowledge you have gained from above, you should be able to help them.

Are You a Forgiving Person?

In our research with the Flourishing Families Project, we asked LDS and non-LDS parents how forgiving they were of themselves and how forgiving they thought other family members were. For example, we asked the teen how forgiving he thought he was in general and then we asked him to rate father and mother on the forgiveness scale.

The findings are important and interesting. The following table shows dads and kids divided into two groups: the scores were reworked so that each person was labeled with regard to how they rated themselves about being a forgiving person. They were asked, "Do you think of yourself as a forgiving person?" They had a six-point scale to respond to that went from "very unforgiving" to "very forgiving."

The first table tells us that dads rated themselves as being remarkably unforgiving. In fact, 36 percent said they were very or mostly unforgiving. However, their kids disagreed. Only 20 percent of those dad's kids said their dads were unforgiving. It didn't matter much if the teen was a boy or girl.

Some LDS dads overall were significantly more likely to rate themselves as unforgiving than non-LDS dads. The big difference was, however, that 38 percent of LDS dads who were reporting on their teen girls said they were unforgiving or very unforgiving. But when we asked their daughters if their dads were unforgiving, only 16 percent said their dads were unforgiving. Dads were more than twice as likely to say they were unforgiving compared to their daughter's ratings of them.

TABLE 1
Dads' rating of themselves as unforgiving compared to how their children rated them

	Total	Boys	Girls
Non-LDS Dads			
Dads of children (by gender) who rate themselves as unforgiving	36%	35%	37%
Children (by gender) who rate their dads as unforgiving	20%	22%	16%
LDS Dads			
Dads of children (by gender) who rate themselves as unforgiving	32%	25%	38%
Children (by gender) who rate their dads as unforgiving	21%	23%	16%

I found the same pattern when looking at how the kids rated their mothers vis-a-vis the mother's reports of themselves. Overall, some parents rate themselves far more harshly on virtues like forgiveness than do their children.

Interestingly, when we asked children to rate themselves and then had the parents rate their children with regard to forgiveness, we found a similar pattern. Non-LDS Children also rated themselves as more unforgiving than did their parents. The difference was not as extreme as when the parents rated themselves compared to their children's ratings. But still, a strong trend in our data is that people rate themselves as more unforgiving than other people see them. In this case, the rating was a close family member who knew the person very well.

One of the interesting findings that didn't fit the above pattern was how LDS children rated themselves compared to how their fathers rated them. In the table below you can see that 29 percent of LDS fathers thought their teen girls were unforgiving. But only 19 percent of those girls said they were unforgiving. The girls thought they were much nicer than their dads did.

TABLE 2
Children's rating of themselves as unforgiving compared to how their dad rated them

	Total	Boys	Girls
Non-LDS Children			
Children (by gender) who rate themselves as unforgiving	29%	28%	27%
Dads who rate their children (by gender) as unforgiving	26%	24%	29%
LDS Children			
Children (by gender) who rate themselves as unforgiving	20%	22%	19%
Dads who rate their children (by gender) as unforgiving	27%	25%	29%

These data tell us three important things about family life and forgiveness. First, there is a pretty good chance you see yourself differently that your children do. As we were going through the data about forgiveness, less than 20 percent of the sample agreed about anyone's forgiveness score. That is true of several other family measures in this study.

The second thing we learn from these data is that children have a different view of the forgiveness process than do their parents, especially the fathers. Forgivingness will be an easier task in families if the family members have a better understanding of what it means to be forgiving. Families will also do better at learning how to forgive when they have a more accurate idea about how they are seen by others. Imagine the disconnect we are seeing as evidenced in the above data.

Back to our family example, Bonnie had a very different view of herself than did her parents and even Alex's parents. She saw herself as a loving and forgiving person, but her dad has very different view of her. He saw her as more impulsive, prone to making poor decisions, and rather unforgiving. This was amplified in the cell phone incident. Once confronted about the issue, she blamed Alex for the whole problem. According to her, Alex should have never passed the picture on. And her father was pretty accurate of his assessment of her as a non-forgiving person. Bonnie essentially never spoke to Alex again. Ed and Jill tried on numerous occasions to use this incident as an example and encouraged Bonnie to forgive. Her hurt, anger, and embarrassment could never be quenched. And her unforgivingness had a dramatic effect on the cohesion of the church group and on her friendships at school. She also hated AJ with a powerful anger that was probably fueled by her embarrassment as well.

The father and the Father. On the other hand, the Brodies seemed to fair pretty well after this episode. For one thing, if Alex had taken our unforgivingness scale, he probably would have rated his dad as pretty forgiving and himself as forgiving as well. Alex understood the principle; it had been taught to him for years not only in family home evening, but, more important, by watching his dad under fire. I am also guessing Alex gained enormous respect for his dad watching him handle the cell phone incident. Alex knew he had done wrong and was committed to doing better. But just as important, he knew his dad had forgiven him.

Alex watched his dad and watched how he considered the incident with calm poise and class. His dad had been upset, but he calmed himself quickly. He had then sought out information and trusted his son's account of what had happened. Then Ethan had acted with reasoned sense that included a strong show of support and love for his child and respect for the others involved. From this example, Alex learned a bit about how his Father in Heaven works.

The final thought is to restate the *As I Have Loved You Principle* and apply it here. That principle indicated that how we, as fathers, act toward our children will be, in great measure, the template and model that our children use to think about their Heavenly Father. That template will last with them always and it is nearly impossible to dislodge that model.

Think of the disconnect when a father says to a child, "You have a loving and caring Father in Heaven" and then when something goes wrong the earthly father is harsh, irrational, prone to overreacting, rude, crude, and out-of control. That's a real and powerful reason for you and I to practice being a forgiving, and therefore a loving, earthly father.

Virtue #5: Sacrifice

Heartbeat Dads Sacrifice for Their Children and Teach Sacrifice to Their Children

Without sacrifice there is no true worship of God. ... "The Father gave His Son, and the Son gave his life," and we do not worship unless we give—give of our substance, ... our time, ... strength, ... talent, ... faith, ... [and] testimonies.
—Teachings of Gordon B. Hinckley [1997], 565

THERE IS PROBABLY NO OTHER FACET OF THE HEART THAT IS MORE connected to family life than is sacrifice. Let's start with a story from one of my students. The following student drawing of her family gives us some interesting insights into how this dad approaches his family—and how he might have been a better leader and example of sacrificing in his family.

Marty[45] told me in her family analysis paper that this picture captures how her family deals with closeness and sacrifice. She began by saying that their family motto was "Love One Another—But No Hugs." In her family, physical connection was not a part of their life, even though they did love one another. She talked about her mother being the real leader in the family. You can see her mother in the top left corner of the heart with a phone. The mom is connected to most of her children. Marty told me that her family was "together but apart." The segments in the heart drawing capture this idea.

The no-hugs family

Notice, however, that the dad has a solid line separating him from the rest of the family except for the mother. She says in her paper, "Dad is kind of irrelevant, we don't talk to him much. And we don't tell him what is going on in our lives. He gets his information from my mom." She went on to describe her father as not invested and not really a part of the daily scene at home. She commented that her father usually attended church with the family and her family is very religious. However, being at church was one of the only activities they did together as a family. She went on to comment that she felt like church attendance was more of a performance about family image rather than a family building activity.

Notice in the drawing that one child doesn't have a phone. One daughter is not active in church activities and is somewhat ostracized from the family. Marty told me that sometimes people talk to Alice, but mostly Alice believes that other family members are always judging her for the choices she has made. According to Marty, Alice doesn't feel a sense of forgiveness or connection—only rejection and condemnation. Marty related how there were only limited attempts to connect with Alice to get her involved in the family.

Sadly, she then characterized her father with money in one hand and a laptop in the other. She wrote in her paper that the children mostly saw him as someone only there for the monetary support and not for daily advice or counsel. The lack of daily investment and sacrifice for his children was a painful concept for Marty to comment on.

She also related how the mother treated the dad like a child instead of a co-parent. She laments in her paper that she has tried to get closer to her dad, but it has been hard to build on something that wasn't there for so many years.

As I think about Marty's family drawing, I can't help but think of the recurring theme of this book: the Savior wants us to show love to others in the same way he shows love to us. This principle surely includes the joy of sacrificing in family life. Simply put, smart dads show love in the same ways Christ demonstrated love to others—by sacrificing for them and putting their interests above their own.

The point is simple: We teach our children about Christlike love when we invest and sacrifice in our children's lives. When we neglect that important mission, we weaken our families. There are two important additions to that idea we will explore here. Sacrificing has to be a regular heartbeat activity. Sporadic and inconsistent sacrifice doesn't work very well. There has to be a significant amount of "floor-time." That is, time spent on the floor playing Scrabble©, looking at books, and watching TV together.

Second, when our sacrifices are more sacred-focused, the power of them is magnified. If we view our children as a part of a larger eternal plan, then sacrificing for them takes on a different texture and meaning.

What Does It Mean to Sacrifice?

The term sacrifice has many meanings. If you look in the dictionary, the first definition usually says something like, "sacrifice is to make something sacred." Originally, the word *sacrifice* came from Latin and first appeared in the mid-thirteenth century.[46] It is a combination of two Latin words: *sacer,* which is the Latin word for something hallowed, holy, or sacred; and *facere,* which is an action word meaning to do something or to perform an act.

Historically, sacrifice meant performing an act that made our efforts holy or sacred. Another way we look at the term *sacrifice* is when holy men would kill an animal or even a human as a gift to the gods. In some ways, that idea may be more linked to the way we want to the use the word *sacrifice* here. A sacrifice makes a demand of us, like giving up a prized animal. A sacrifice means we give up something important to us for something else that we think is of higher value. Giving a sacred sacrifice means giving up something important for something else *and* we do it with the idea that that act has a sacred meaning or a result that is spiritual or holy.

So, when we hear the word *sacrifice*, we usually think about giving up something we treasure or is special to us like money, sleep, comfort, space, or time for something we think will be a better outcome for ourselves or others. For example, we could "sacrifice" some space in the garage until our teen's birthday while a special present is kept there under wraps. Franklin, the teen getting the special present, sees the large covered object in the garage and knows it is probably for his birthday. Brent, the dad is doing a little bit of sacrifice, because the weather has changed and there is a definite chance of snow. Brent has to park his car on the street for two weeks. The thing that makes this example work is that Brent gave up something he valued—getting into a warm car that isn't covered in ice. He is going to be parking on the street and scraping ice.

Let's take the example one step further. The sacrifice becomes sacred when we think bigger and in terms of a sacred goal or ideal. Back to the garage: Brent knows that Betty has been struggling with Franklin. They have been arguing more lately and their relationship is strained. Brent has a strong feeling about the eternal nature of families and believes that his relationship with his son is an eternally lasting association. He also was amazed at the gift Betty had imagined; the gift wasn't expensive, but is was very thoughtful and also reflects Betty's ideal that her relationship with Franklin is infinitely more important than nearly anything in her life. She is hoping this gift will help show her love for Franklin and get them talking again.

The story of the garage and the gift has transformed. Brent and

Betty both are thinking in more sacred ways and are considering a larger more eternal view of the situation. Even though it is an ordinary event and even though it is for a short period of time, Brent's thinking was different. When he came out each morning, even the morning when there was a ton of snow on his car, his response to the small but powerful sacrifice was different: he was more patient; it gave him a chance to remember for just a moment how much his wife loved their son; he also thought for a minute about how much his son meant to him. In this case, Brent could take the longer view and as he did that the ice-trouble melted away.

Several years ago, Robert Bellah and his colleagues wrote a book called, *Habits of the Heart.* In this book, he argued that there is a trend to emphasize individualism and personal freedom over relationships that require commitment, obligation, and sacrifice. In fact, his claim was that the notion of sacrificing for others was seriously fading. In this book, the authors asked several hundred couples what they thought about sacrifice in marriage:

Even the most secure, happily married of our respondents had difficulty when they sought a language [to talk about why they were married] that went beyond the self... they resisted the notion that such relationships might involve obligations ... and they were troubled by the ideal of self-denial the term "sacrifice" implied.[47]

In our Flourishing Families Project, we also asked about sacrifice. We wanted to know how much couples were willing to sacrifice for each other. We couldn't measure their actual sacrificing acts, but we could ask them about the idea. Here are the questions we asked couples about their marriage. Answer the questions in the box below and jot down any thoughts you have about this idea before looking at what other couples said about sacrifice.[48]

Activity: A Questionnaire on Sacrifice

(These question were developed by Markman, et al (1995) and also used in the Flourishing Families Project. I have reworded them slightly). Use the following scale for each question:

How much do you agree with the following statements?

1=strongly disagree
2=disagree
3=somewhat disagree
4=undecided
5=somewhat agree
6=agree
7=strongly agree

_____ 1. Giving up something for my partner means a lot to me.

_____ 2. It can be personally fulfilling to give something up for my partner

_____ 3. I get satisfaction out of doing things for my partner, even if it means I miss out on something I want for myself.

_____ 4. It makes me feel good to sacrifice for my partner.

Add up your score here:
1.
2.
3.
4.

Now divide your score by four and put the result here: _____

Your thoughts:

_____

_____

_____

_____

_____

The Flourishing Families couples completed the survey you see above. The fathers in that sample averaged 5.8. It is interesting to note that over a five-year period, as these dads' teenagers go from about eleven years old to sixteen years old, his score dropped significantly—almost one whole point on this scale. The mother's scores also dropped steeply as the child entered the teen years. We aren't going to spend a lot of time on that idea in this book, but there are some significant effects as teens pass from middle school into high school. Relationships become a bit more strained overall, and parents may not feel like being as sacrificing or charitable.

Our job as fathers is to fight that trend. If anything, the emerging teen years are the time to boost our efforts. Our default position may be to push back, push away, hide, and disengage when things get troubling. One way to fight back and not push away is to try doses of daily and ordinary sacrifice for our children.

Dads and extraordinary sacrifice. Most of the time when we hear stories about sacrifice in family life it is dramatic. For example, I heard recently of a family member who gave another family member a kidney. That act of love seems to qualify as a sacrifice. Person A gave person B something they really, really liked having (a kidney, for example) for the benefit of someone else. We celebrate and love to hear those examples. I knew a father once who had scrimped and saved for years so his son could go on a mission. The day he wrote the check for the mission was very emotional. I don't want to put a damper on those kinds of *extraordinary* sacrifices. They are amazing, and we all love to hear about them. But there is another kind of sacrifice that is not featured enough in our stories about men in families; we don't think about the *ordinary* sacrifices parents make.

A close friend of mine recently relayed the story of his son to me. Early in his boy's life, it was discovered that his son had muscular dystrophy. The family watched as his muscles became weaker and weaker. Christian eventually died from the disease at age twenty-three.

Before his death, however, this caring dad related to me how challenging it was to see Christian's body gradually become weaker. There were many sacrifices that had to be made. For example, the family decided to build a house. The design of the house didn't begin in the kitchen or with the patio or even the living rooms in mind. Instead, at the core of the house was an elevator for Christian that would take him from the main area in the house to the basement where his bedroom was. The cost of the elevator was substantial and other features of the home had to be adjusted.

Christian's health problems affected the whole family. Gary, the dad, recalled one day in particular, "Christian was in the third grade and his older brother was in the fifth grade. Their elementary school was about four blocks from our home. Christian wore leg braces at the time, and could still walk, but as I looked out the window, I saw Kyle carrying Christian on his shoulders. I was so touched as I watched. After they came home, I told Kyle how much I appreciated the ways he helped Christian."

According to Gary, Kyle just looked at his dad and said, "Well . . . he's my brother." You could tell by the way Gary told this story, many years after it had happened that it was still an emotional event for him.

Gary also told me how Christian's illness helped all of the family learn patience, service, caring, consideration, and love . . . and also appreciation and gratitude in ways that could have never happened without this challenge being a part of their lives.

Gary related another feature of this story that is very important. He spoke very reverentially about those difficult years and how, at the time, their family was immersed in not only Christian's illness, but also in serving tirelessly for the Muscular Dystrophy Association.

Gary went on to explain that when Christian was still alive, they were more aware of the sadness of Christian's situation and how those challenges brought blessings to their family. But time has given greater clarity to this family, and as the years have passed, Gary commented that they have come to an even clearer understanding of the many blessings Christian's illness brought to their family.

His final comment to me was very touching. Gary said, "Even though there were many difficult sacrifices during those years, the blessings he and his situation brought were so much more important that we cherish the opportunity we had to have him in our home."

The following picture was taken at our local cemetery. The loving inscriptions and the constant flowers that appear there long after the death of the young boy attest to the love and sacrifice parents make for their children.

A loving parent placed this memorial to his son who died at an early age

Sacred sacrifices and our motivations. At the heart of sacrifice is how to think of sacrifice differently. On the one hand, we may have the idea of sacrifice as a primarily self-centered act of becoming a more disciplined runner or sacrificing garage space because we have been asked to help out. On the other hand, we have acts of sacrifice that are somehow sacred in nature. The first way to tell one type of sacrifice from the other is to think about motivation: why are you and I doing something? Here are some typical motivations to choose from.

Let's think back for a minute on the example of Gary and his disabled son. He and his wife made some choices when they were building their house. One key choice was that they had to put an elevator in the house so Christian could easily have access to the entire house. So, why did he do that? I think I know a little about why Gary did this, but first let's examine some other possible reasons (not Gary's) that had the same result.

One reason we do things is because we look down the road and it seems to us it would be better to do something now rather than to have to be bothered with the problem over and over again in the future. Let's call this motivation the *avoiding future pain*. In this case, building the elevator for his son wouldn't really be about this act as an example of Christlike love and genuine concern for someone else. Nah—this type of motivation is really about us thinking about future cost. "If I don't build the elevator, I am going to be the one, because I'm the dad, carrying Christian up and down the stairs every time there is a special occasion in the basement and every time he wants to have a friend over to watch TV."

Another type of motivation that isn't really about sacrifice is when we are trying to please someone else. The center of the motivation is, again, really not about our actual love for the child, but instead it is about us feeling good that someone thinks we are a good person. So, if this were the case, Gary might be thinking to himself, "I am going to build this elevator at great cost, but you know what? People are going to think I am a great dad for that. In fact, another benefit will be that my wife will also think I am a hero." This type of motivation is common, but it isn't as much about sacrifice as it is about a personal agenda. Most of us find ourselves doing things for our family members and others because we want them to see us as "good guys." And, I hasten to add, that is okay—it's a good thing. But it doesn't capture the idea of a sacred sacrifice. Sacrifice is about intentional acts of giving that reflect a more holy or sacred motivation—and I am coming to what those are in a minute.

Another reason Gary might have installed the elevator is for *displaying and showing off.* Occasionally, I see acts of sacrifice that seem like the actor is showing off. In this case, Gary would install the elevator and he would make sure it was by the front door of the house—but not for convenience. Somewhere in the secret parts of his thinking, he had a brief daydream about all the people that would come to visit. And they would have to pass by the elevator, and they would say, "What's that, Gary?" He would say, "That is for our disabled son." The neighbor would say, "Oh my heck, you are the most sacrificing, loving father I have ever met!"

Well, that is a cynical and overcooked example, but sometimes our motivations are carefully designed to look like sacrifice, when in fact there is something else lurking in a dark corner. The problem is that our close family members, especially children, are very good at detecting that kind of disingenuous performance—they know better and we aren't fooling anyone, really.

Another motivation to consider is *the obedience/rule orientation*. In this type of motivation the individual is focused on the rule. Of course being obedient is a good idea and having rules to follow is important. But, in my opinion, obedience is a strategy to use as we are seeking higher and more sacred-based goals. Following the rules is not the goal all by itself—there is a reason why a rule is being followed. Someone who is a rule-oriented, obedient father might say something like, "Della, it is important that we be as obedient as possible in this decision. We have been commanded to be nice to others, and I think it would be a nice thing to do to build an elevator to fulfill our obligation to be nice to family members." Again, my dialogue here is a bit over-the-top. But do you get the idea? The father is, again, focusing on his own salvation and his own need to follow rules is the reason for the action. The overwhelming focus is not on his love for the child and building the elevator as a truly selfless act.

The following principle captures the idea that sacrifice becomes more powerful when the motivation comes from a sacred way of thinking. I don't believe God is motivated to be a part of our lives because He is fearful of censor from another; nor does He seem motivated by self-interest. In my view, He is a part of our lives first and foremost because He loves us and wants us to succeed. He seeks our joy and salvation.

Principle #14: True Sacrificing Is a Holy Act

When we sacrifice for someone else and the goal is to enrich his or her life, the act becomes holy and sacred. When we do something for someone else and the real reason is to boost self-interest, then the act is ordinary and not as sacred.

Extraordinary sacrifice. Heartbeat fathers sacrifice on a regular basis and usually in simple ways. This type of common and ordinary sacrifice has to do with spending time on the floor with our children playing games, watching TV, helping with homework, hearing their stories of friends, and helping them solve problems.

Nick's example. I was having lunch with a friend not long ago. I know Nick is an avid sports fan. He has a son who wants terribly to be a college basketball player. Nick is helping him because Nick is a very good basketball player himself and coaches kids every season. Nick was explaining to me that his son, Nathan, just turned fourteen and is turning up the heat to get ready to be a "star" in the high school team. Nathan has the talent and persistent drive to actually do this, But Nick has decided that he shouldn't push Nathan too hard. Nick has realized that his relationship with Nathan is far more important than Nathan possibly becoming an NBA player. He talked at length about other fathers he knows who push their kids at sports with unrelenting pressure.

We started talking about the notion of sacrifice and what it really means. Nick gave me an example that hits this principle square on the head. His orientation and core ideals are first about his relationship with Nathan, not about himself. It was clear as he talked that he would, of course, be proud if Nathan played basketball at the high school in a couple of years. But you could tell that it wasn't about Nick stroking his own ego, having his friends rate him as "father of the year," or about how he would feel at all. There was a genuine love and sparkle in his eye as he talked about how much he loved going with Nathan to the gym every morning before school and working to shoot three hundred baskets. Nick rebounds for Nathan while he practices his jump shots.

Then he told of an example that really hit home. I asked Nick if there was ever a problem of not wanting to go to the gym at 5:00 a.m. every morning. I also was probing a bit and asked him how hard it was to get Nathan out of bed every morning. My sneakiness was a cleaver disguise for wanting to find out why Nick was "really" doing this. I was surprised when Nick related that he had told Nate this year that the basketball practice had to come from Nate and not from him (Nick). And that if they were going to continue with the 5:00 a.m. basketball, Nate would have to be the one to get himself up and then come in and wake up Nick.

I asked again, "Don't you ever just want to 'not go'?" Nick looked at me with true love in his eyes as he explained that the time he spent with Nate was priceless. We joked about the MasterCard commercial. "Trip to Disneyland, $3,500; souvenirs at Sea World, $250; an hour in the morning playing basketball with a fourteen-year-old—priceless."

Nick also told me that often in those few minutes in the morning Nate would share and connect with him about problems he was having or issues he was worried about. Then, he related a key story about this arrangement. Nick said that about a week ago, he had been up all night with a pretty bad headache. He had been turning and tossing all night and had just fallen asleep when Nate tugged on his arm. He thought for just a moment about saying, "Not today, buddy—I really don't feel well." But he didn't say that. Instead, he rolled out of bed and they drove to the gym. Nick ended the story by making sure I knew that nothing spectacular happened that day at the gym that would change Nate's life forever. He wasn't telling me the story to let me know he was, "the greatest dad in the world."

I jumped in and said that this story told me that something extraordinary did happen that day. That single act of rolling out of bed when it would have been easier to let it go was a true and holy sacrifice. He was investing in his son and putting his own needs in the background. In truth, it is probably impossible to do things for others with absolutely no thought of our own wants and needs. The true principle of sacrifice, however, asks us to put those needs second, at least.

I finished the conversation by asking Nick, "Why did you do that when you were sick?" His answer was simple and on-point, "Well" he said slowly, "I love being a part of Nate's life." What an A-plus answer. It seems to me that Heavenly Father says the same thing to us: "I want to be a part of your life and help you out in any way I can."

These types of "ordinary" stories are what life is all about. The stories I like the most are about the everyday *quotidian*. The word quotidian is about the powerful but ordinary events of our lives. The everyday small things that happen are often the most meaningful.

Principle #15: Ordinary Sacrifice

Ordinary sacrifice is as important, if not more
important, than more dramatic, extraordinary sacrifices.

JOURNAL OF THOUGHTS
Why do you sacrifice?

This is a more difficult journal entry that requires a bit of self-inspection. In this chapter there were several different types of motivations for acts of love described. First, think of a time when you did something for your child that was honestly because you loved them and wanted to be a part of his or her life.

What was the event?

_____

_____

Do you remember how it felt to be a part of that event? Describe your thoughts and feelings.

_____

_____

_____

_____

_____

_____

Can you think of other times when you have done something for your children and it was to just follow the rule, not get in trouble for not doing it, or for some other reason that was more based on your interest than on the child's? Write that down here—with some explanation about how it went (at least you were there and trying, right?).

_____

_____

_____

The real heroic dads are those who focus on the quotidian and realize that the daily selfless acts toward another are the building blocks of truly sacred sacrifice. It is the everyday small events of our lives that will make the overall large-scale differences in the lives of our children.

Megan's family. Sacrificing is sometimes difficult for families. The following is another family drawing from a student in one of my classes. Look at the drawing below of the Franks Family. What do you see?

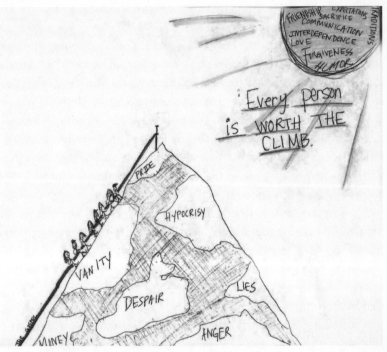

Megan's family seems to be a typical family; she started her paper by showing that her family has strengths and weaknesses. I have each student decide what they think is the motto for their family. I especially like this motto that she came up with: "Each Person is Worth Climbing For." She explained in her paper that each family member had challenges and problems, but she said that their family was unwilling to leave anyone behind. The first struggle Megan talked about was money. Her family was in debt and battled to keep bread on the table. How to spend and save money is a key element of this family.

I found it interesting that as she talked about money issues in her family, there wasn't a sense of blame or hostility about past wrongs. Instead, she recognized that her family had this problem and all members were doing their part to climb that mountain. It was clear in her paper that the dad was leading the way in this climb. Notice that he is in front leading the group. Compare that to the family drawing we saw first. In that family analysis, Marty lamented that her father was "like a child in the family" and he didn't sacrifice or lead for them much at all. In this paper, Megan shows her father leading the pack, putting his own interests second to that of the needs of his family.

Megan told me that her father had a goal of becoming financially independent. But she was quick to add that he saw the financial independence as a sacred-based sacrifice. By that she meant that they weren't trying to get out of debt so they could build a bigger home or buy a better ski-boat. Instead, the goal was to become economically free from debts. The sacrifices they were making were not driven by wealth accumulation for its own sake. Instead, she talked about how her parents wanted to help their children through school and then eventually go on missions themselves.

She spent several paragraphs in her paper talking about how their family had made a clear ideological shift from heading down the wrong trail of materialism, greed, and "vanity." She says, "The children in my family have spent too many years focusing on making smart financial moves…at the expense of focusing on other things that matter more."

She also described how her mother was a champion "screamer" and her father was prone to occasional "explosive outbursts." But, she then wrote about how they have tried to use the principles of sacrifice, humor, love, and forgiveness to get to a better place in their family life. Notice that these virtues are part of the "sunshine" in the top corner. She was very clear that her family found direction by trying to become more loving, forgiving, and sacrificing instead of focused on hypocrisy and materialism.

I think this story is an excellent example. All of us have mountains to climb in family life. As Megan attested, her family was able to do a better job of beating the problems they faced. And I also loved her story because the dad took the lead.

Applying These Principles

The trick to being a successful father is, of course, in the application: the first practical application from the above principles is that in order to teach children about sacred, heartbeat-style sacrifice, you have to use that idea yourself. The Heartbeat type of fathering includes the daily sacrifices. It is about the power of the quotidian in our lives. Your children need to see you spending time with them. It should be regular and it can't be only time set aside as FHE teaching time, or time when you are delegated to discipline someone.

Avoid being the Disneyland Daddy. It is certainly okay to plan big events, but if that is the only time you have to spend with a child, then it may be seen as a shallow and vapid form of investment.

Find someone or something that you can do with them that isn't about getting a merit badge or filling a young men's requirement or service project to check off. Consider something that lasts for several months—here are some examples:

A book drive for your local library—that is not an Eagle project

Finding a neighbor who needs regular yard work or help with dinners or just needs a friend

Consider working for Habitat for Humanity. They are always looking for volunteers.

Demonstrate your love to your spouse by sacrificing for her. Try to find moments throughout the week when you could surrender up something important to you so that she could do something she needs or want to do.

Teach a child to be involved in the life of one of their siblings—not for a day, not as a secret Santa, not as a gimmick that lasts over the weekend. But something that is more long term. Maybe you could have a weekly meeting with the child and help them plan how to become an invested, interested, intentional, and loving part of another family member's life.

All of this requires that you be intentional on this aspect of loving. These expressions of love won't happen accidently or in the course of life without your direction—preside. Presiding means you are intentional about the agenda of what needs to be done.

Activity: Teaching Sacrifice in FHE

You have plenty of content to build a couple of strong FHE experiences about sacrifice. After talking about some of the topics covered here, see if family members have any ideas of how your family can sacrifice for each other on a daily basis.

You may want to show the movie *Chariots of Fire*. This is an inspirational movie about Eric Liddell. He was an Olympic runner in the 1920s and made several heroic decisions about running on Sundays. The more interesting part of this story is about Eric's life after the Olympics not examined in the movie. He became a missionary for his church in the turbulence prior to World War II. His missionary experiences in China are particularly telling about a man who gave his life for what he believed. There are several short biographies about his life that can help you teach his story.

Activity: Building a Family Flag

Have your family take a stab at making a family flag. You saw examples earlier that will help you know more about what your family thinks about your family. Here are the steps I tell my students when they are building a flag.

First have family members work together to come up with a motto. Read them several mottos that are possibilities. You can find lists of mottos on the Internet. It is important in this activity that the parents not dominate the conversation. The family picture or family flag should represent everyone's view.

Show a couple of examples of pictures you have seen in this book to demonstrate as examples.

Give each family member a space to work alone, paper and other art supplies, and about twenty minutes to work on a drawing. Give them the following directions:
A picture of our family is a personal thing. If you don't want to share it with the others family members, that is okay. We are going to work

separately and draw a picture that tells what our family is like. Make sure you put in all the family members somewhere on your drawing. You could even put pets if you want and other family members that are not living here. Your picture is a kind of flag or map about what your family does and what it means to you.

Once everyone is done. Have those who want to share their pictures talk about what their family means to them.

You may want to take the activity a step further and see if you can get some consensus about a group flag. I know several families who have actually made a quilted family flag with symbols and mottos that capture who they are and what is important to them.

PFI: Family Flag

Sometime after this family activity about the flag and family motto, schedule a few minutes with the target child—or children. Have them bring their family flag to the Personal Father Interview. Encourage them to talk about how they see your family. It is critical that you don't "correct" or challenge their view: it is their view and your job is to learn from it.

You may want to share with them your view of the family. Again, this is not an opportunity to say your view is the right view and theirs is wrong. Try focusing on the positive elements of your family and let them know what you see as family strengths.

In the following Journal of Thoughts, record what you discovered.

JOURNAL OF THOUGHTS
Family flag activity report

In this JOT, record how the Person Father Interview went with your child about the family. What did you learn? What type of emotional feeling was present? Did you have any "strokes of ideas" as you were talking about the core beliefs of your family and how your child sees your family?

_____

_____

_____

_____

_____

_____

_____

_____

_____

_____

_____

_____

_____

_____

_____

_____

_____

_____

_____

_____

_____

Virtue #6:
Harmony and Peace
Heartbeat Dads Find and Teach Harmony
instead of Contention

When we feel anger or contention in our homes, we should immediately recognize what power has taken control of our lives and what Satan is endeavoring to accomplish. Solomon provided us this wise formula: 'A soft answer turneth away wrath: but grievous words stir up anger' (Prov. 15:1). Our home should ideally be a refuge where each member feels safe, secure, loved, and insulated from harsh criticism and contention that we so often encounter in the world.
—Elder Wayne S. Peterson

CONTENTION IS HELL IN FAMILIES. CONTROVERSIES, STRUGGLES, tussles, disagreements, and quarrels are inevitable, especially in family life. But when the kerfuffle escalates to contention, real trouble follows. The fact is that struggle is necessary for healthy relationships. When there are two competing ideas of similar worth, we tussle a bit to see which of those ideas makes the most sense. However, struggle occasionally turns to strife, dissension, argument, and conflict. Conflict in family relationships includes a wide range of behaviors, including verbal aggression, hostility, enmity, antagonism, and even hate. The topic here is about eliminating conflict and inviting the spirit of harmony into our families. Avoiding conflict is a good first step toward developing harmony, but the absence of contention does not guarantee harmony. The spirit of harmony has to be fought for. Sounds odd, doesn't it—you have to fight to have harmony? Like all of the virtues in this book, harmony doesn't come easy; it has to be worked for and fought for.

Scriptural Foundation for Avoiding Contention

Let's begin with some word play and a couple of key scriptures about contention and conflict. Too often I hear people throwing words around that sound like the right thing to say but, in fact, the word they are using really isn't the word they think they are using. Here is a good example: the word *contention* is often used instead of the word *struggle*. Contention is about struggle. But when struggle produces strife, contention follows. As I said above, struggle in families is inevitable; strife, however, is a different animal. It is defined as bitter conflict, quarreling, and fighting with the purpose of making another person do something they may not want to do by controlling or harming them. A struggle can start out innocently, but it turns to war when negotiations break and the talking is over.

It is interesting to note how much emphasis the Savior places on contention. When Jesus visited the people in 3 Nephi 11:21–27, contention was the second thing he talked about. The first thing he taught the people when he visited them was the power of baptism and committing to the cause. The next thing he introduced was not church organization nor elaborations on doctrine. Instead, the second thing he insisted (3 Nephi 11:28–29) was that they stop the disputations and contention. By definition a disputation is a verbal controversy. He insisted that they stop the arguing and verbal battling. He then reminded his flock that verbal battles are a tool of the devil, who is the father of contention. By verbally battling we invite Satan into our lives; Satan is the master of stirring up our hearts and the result is contention.

It seems to me he is saying, "Unless you can stop the verbal battles, I will have to depart." That is a key idea in 3 Nephi. He reminds the people that having verbal battles is not His doctrine and that such things should be done away with immediately. As in those times, I believe the Savior cannot remain and be an integral part of our lives when we are caught up in verbal battles (disputations) that lead to contention (struggle and opposition that have the element of strife attached).

Remember the "strokes of ideas" principle. This idea is reinforced in D&C 121:26 with the following statement: "*God shall give you knowledge by his Holy Spirit, ye, by the unspeakable gift of the Holy*

Ghost . . ." If we are to have the inspiration and strokes of ideas we so desperately need to be good parents, then we cannot do anything that will chase the Spirit from our presence.

Principle #16: Harmony and Strokes of Ideas

The Spirit of the Lord cannot be a part of our lives
when we are involved in contentious relationships
with others, including family members.

This theme reappears frequently in sacred texts including conference talks but none as open and direct as in D&C 121. In the last verses of D&C 121, the Lord speaks boldly about those who would use their powers unwisely in the world. It seems to me that this last part of D&C 121 is a manual for relationship building. There is a clear statement about how not to destroy relationships within Church government, at work, or especially within family life.

Read D&C 121:37. The words *control, domination,* and *compulsion* are carefully chosen and emphasized in this verse. Notice that commas in the original do not separate these three words, as you would expect. The verse says, "control **or** dominion **or** compulsion." This is an important grammatical strategy to make sure the reader gets the message that these are separate and distinct ideas. Most of us read this text thinking those three words are synonyms. Let's look at them more carefully.

Control is a very powerful word. The term *control* means to exercise or put into action a restraining influence over someone. In other words, control is about restraint. Restraining someone is about checking his actions—think of a hockey player slamming someone up against the glass in a "body-check." The other player wants to head toward the goal and the opposing player doesn't want him to, so he gives him a body-slam against the glass to disrupt the play.

Domination or dominion means that we would see ourselves as dominant. That is, we seek ultimate influence. We use power to show, demonstrate, and insist that our ideas will be the ones adhered to. As I read the scriptures, a father's job with his children—especially teenagers—is not to reign with terror, power, and control. Instead, our job is more about being responsible, involved, and an attentive gardener. By being an effective gardener parent instead of dominating with an iron-fist, we work instead for liberation, self-direction, contribution, a sense of joint venture, emancipation, and enfranchisement.

When domination is more prevalent we are much more likely to engage in disenfranchisement, marginalization, exclusion, and alienation. Domination and alienation seem to go hand-in-hand. That is probably why Satan likes us to buy into that idea. When one dominates another, most of us push back and want to steer our own course. The more one is dominated, the more we want to be clear of that person.

Compulsion is the final element in this unholy trifecta. Compulsion is usually defined as an irresistible and persistent impulse to make someone do something he doesn't want to do. So, with regard to fathering, control is keeping children from doing things they want to do. Domination is forcing our world ideology on children even when they don't like it. And compulsion is the final blow to a relationship when a father forces a child to do something he thinks she should do but she doesn't really want to.

In family life, our job as parents is, of course, to limit, direct, counsel, advise, and guide. This scripture says that we step out-of-bounds when we control another person in "unrighteousness." That is, we are making someone—in our case, a teenager—do something he doesn't want to do and we want him to do it because we have tainted and selfish goals.

Let's try an example. Justin is your fourteen-year-old son. He has been very good about going to church and doing his homework in the past. Lately, however, he has decided that he would rather not go to church but wants to sleep in instead. Your attempts to persuade, advise, counsel, and teach don't seem to be working. This struggle (he has one thing in mind and you have another) is turning toward contention, and strife begins to arise when your anger rises—if for no other reason, than he is defying your wishes. It becomes contentious when the negotiations break down and you roll out the big guns and start a war—or maybe he is the one who hurls the first stone— regardless, struggles sometimes lead to strife and then to war.

In addition, Justin has a responsibility at church that he refuses to attend to. To make things worse, the bishop has talked to you about Justin's attitude in the teacher's quorum meeting. Your wife is deeply concerned about Justin's "tone" and is asking you to do something about the direction in which things seem to be headed. Let's focus here on your response to Justin's defiance. In order to come up with a sound response strategy, you will need "strokes of ideas" about how to cope with this situation and to begin to build a response. To get those strokes of ideas, you will need to approach a problem like this from a position of harmony and an open heart. Approaching it with a heart filled with contention, control, domination, and compulsion will only make the situation worse. Your job is to persuade, counsel, connect, problem solve, and show interest. Sure, I'll bet you could actually "make" him go to church. You could use threats, take away so many privileges that he would buckle, or you could even physically drag him there. If you use those strategies, chances are you will not enjoy the unintended results of relationship damage. His obedience to a principle has to come from his heart—not your belt.

Remember, we are exploring how to promote harmony and avoid contention. Your entry point into being able to solve this situation is first doing no harm. And second, you have to approach this from a harmonious, non-contentious approach. Again, if you don't, it will only escalate and lead to the worst kind of contention we usually deal with—contention in the home.

Harm comes in many forms; exercising control when motivated by fear, embarrassment, intimidation, rage, anger, indignation, anxiety, or even deep concern won't work. The reason it won't work is clear. When we control people (such as make them do something they don't want to do that we think they should do), we had better be sure it is not because we are acting out of self-interest. You may need to exert some control—but only if prompted to do so. Your actions will be different if you put the fear and anxiety aside (that may be hard) and focus primarily on the relationship, and Justin's motivation for not wanting to go to church.

I occasionally hear of dads who turn up the control volume because they claim to have been prompted to do so. I am sure there may be occasions when that is the case. In my experience, however, it often seems to me that the worse situation is when a parent feels out-of-control, is panicky, embarrassed, and hurt—and they turn up of the control-volume dial as a way to solve things and, at the same time, claim it is inspired so no one will question their motives. That strategy seems to fly directly against the counsel given in D&C 121. Whenever we use control, dominion, and compulsion, we had better be sure it is actually the Spirit prompting us and not away to fulfill our needs or even our own short-comings.

I have been a father (and now grandfather) for forty-three years and can only think of two to three instances when the use of control or compulsion were ever a clear prompting that needed to be acted upon. I have had numerous times that my children's decisions have caused pain, embarrassment, grief, and anger. And there have been plenty of times when I have rolled out the big guns of control, compulsion, and even retribution. But whenever I have acted as a father using those deadly tools, it usually has been to serve my own grief or to relieve my own pain or embarrassment. To be honest, the Spirit rarely asks us to cut someone's head off (like the story of Nephi and Laban). In fact, those incidences are so rare, they end up as featured stories in ancient texts. The more common occurrence is that when we act like men usually do when attempting to cover sins or respond to feelings of hurt pride, we lash out. The unfortunate results are damage to the relationship, and the Spirit of the Lord is grieved and withdraws. The obvious tragedy of that situation is clear: like the Spirit, our child also pulls away *and* the much-needed strokes of ideas we need are withdrawn. So we are left on our own to solve the problem without help.

Elder Jeffrey R. Holland said, "Some things we say can be destructive, even venomous—and that is a chilling indictment for a Latter-day Saint! The voice that bears profound testimony, utters fervent prayer, and sings the hymns of Zion *can be* the same voice that berates and criticizes, embarrasses and demeans, inflicts pain and destroys the spirit of oneself and of others in the process."[49]

As I said earlier, some dads have a mistaken idea that becoming a drill-sergeant is their right and the preferred way to get children ready for the world. But most dads, in my opinion, who use a contention-based parenting approach are mostly embarrassed at prospective failure or genuinely overanxious in their attempts to do what they think is right.

Take a look at the following picture and see if you can decipher what is happening.

This picture is from a family analysis paper written by a student several years ago. She drew the picture above to help describe the core beliefs of her family. The father in this picture is drawn in the middle. He is the one whose eyes are sad and the word GOD is the first thing you see on his face. She wrote that her father thought of himself as God in the family but in a very controlling, dictatorial way. Early in this book, I suggested that fathers may be the first encounter children have with someone who is like God. In this case the version of God that this father chose to replicate in the family was a god of fear, control, and humiliation.

She felt her father really did love the family (hence the heart for a mouth) but she drew a chain around the heart and explained that he couldn't really express that love. The mother in this drawing is trying to put on a good face. The student wrote about how the mother was constantly trying to show the ward and local neighborhood that they were a model family. She is also scratching the face of the dad; the student talked about how the mother would, occasionally, strike back with hurt and anger toward the father. According to this student, there were high levels of hostility between the mother and father, and the mother would frequently lash out at his attempts to control and smother everyone.

You can see that with one hand the father is squeezing the life out of three children who are begging for help from God. Another child is being squashed by the large shoe. The student wrote that this child had gone against the dad and stood up to him. The father turned up the compulsion and control to the point of literally squeezing the life out of this son. The child turned against the family, Church, and God.

The broken key on the left bottom corner represented the loss of any solutions, according to this student-artist. She felt like there was no hope. You see her crawling on the ground trying to reach out to other family members who have fled the tyranny of this king-father.

I don't often see these kinds of family analysis papers. But, over the years, I usually find that about 10 percent of my students draw pictures something like the one above and have a heart-wrenching story about abusive or over-intrusive parenting. Let's look at another example where contention has gone over the edge in a family.

You can see a similar theme in the drawing above. This father is being portrayed as the pirate king in his family. The student wrote that a key element in this family was the duplicity of what the father was doing. On the one hand, he was preaching to his family that he believed in charity, compassion, patience, faith, and hope. But in reality, according to this family member, he was using Gospel principles to promote a "reign-of-terror," as the student labeled it. On the left side of the book, we find the "Doctrine of Dad." The family was to pray together, have scripture study, work hard, be obedient, and sacrifice. On the right side of the book is the interpretation of what this student thought the left side really meant.

The true colors of this dad, as drawn by his child, was a daily routine of criticism, manipulation, and fear that created a sense of low worth and feelings of not being really loved. Of course, the drawing of the mother in this situation (she is dangling over the side) is shocking. She is on a leash trying to reach out to her children, who are the beasts of burden for the doctrines of the father. You can see one child—the oldest—waving good-bye in the bottom right. He had had enough.

The women standing behind the father was the grandmother, who had the real control of this family. She was calling all of the shots and had the father on a pretty short leash. These two pictures are not the ones you want your children to take with them when they leave home. These pictures convey the idea of *animosity*. Animosity is about resentment and ill will that becomes active. Animosity is not just about disliking someone or irritation. It is an active desire to do harm.

Bitterness is one step further down this road to war. It is also defined as an active and spirited desire to do harm. When we travel down this road even further, we run into words like *enmity*, which connotes a mutual hatred. And *hate* is really a strong word that means we have a highly developed sense of *disgust* when something is repugnant.

The final word I often hear when people are angry is *contempt* which is also an action word. It is about the act of despising someone whom we have no respect for. As we unravel and dig deep into the sludge of contention, I hope you can see how toxic and menacing it can be. Children don't forget the acid burn scars from this type of toxin in family life.

So, the first step in promoting more harmony at home is removing the toxic waste of contention, domination, control, and compulsion. But that is only the first step. I am not saying that removing this type of toxic relational waste will mean that Justin will suddenly want to go to church, finish his Eagle project, start preparing for his mission, and get accepted to BYU or Stanford. That is not the point. The main point is that you really won't have a chance of building a long lasting celestial-style relationship with your child until you clear out the toxic relational waste.

The two-edged sword principle. The point of this approach is a two-edged sword. As teens begin the process, our job is to teach, connect, counsel, protect, love, and guide. If you promote contention as a way to solve differences in your relationships, you are decreasing the chances of coming up with long-lasting solutions that will result in long-lasting relationships. You can force no child to heaven.

Principle #17: The Two-Edged Sword Principle

Removing the toxic relational waste of control, domination, and compulsion means you are willing to allow children to make age-appropriate decisions. We should never be willing to destroy the relationship for the sake of expected performance.

The Harmony and Unity Side of the Page

Read the description and then look at the picture of a student's family flag, made a couple of years ago:

It seems that our most important family rules have to do with the sacredness of the home. family home evening happens every Monday NO MATTER WHAT, as well as daily family prayer and scripture study. If there is fighting in the home and the individual refuses to stop yelling, they get to resolve their issues in the garage, so as to not disrupt the spirit in the home . . . I have noticed that my mom constantly has spiritual music in the main rooms. I love this about our family, and hope to continue this in my own home.

She goes on to say that a primary theme in their home was cleanliness—you can see that reflected by the toilet-cleaning going on in the picture. Her mother was very picky and you can see the "#5" by the toilet for how many times she had to re-do her cleaning efforts.

She went on to comment that it was the mother that usually set the tone in the home and designed and led family home evening.

Here is another student's description of a time when her dad took the leadership role and found a way to keep the children from quarreling on the way to a special vacation.

I drew a big U in the middle of the heart to represent unity. We often lack harmony in our home and it always sucks when there is contention and disagreement. I feel like when one person is in a bad mood, then everyone becomes in a bad mood. It is like the domino effect and nothing can stop it once it starts. We also start to take sides when contention is formed. We form these triangles between my mom and dad and it just makes things worse.

A lot of times some of my family members overreact making things even more chaotic. Once this happens, it just evolves into a huge chain of unnecessary events that do not help the situation at all. I do not know what the problem is and why we fight so much. I really just want my family to be unified and be a family who can do stuff together without someone getting upset about something. I remember this past summer when my family and I drove to California. We were going to Disneyland and then to my grandparents' house. I remember the car ride so well. Most twelve-hour car rides consist of bickering, complaining, and the occasional screaming. I have sisters the age of nine and ten, and then twin sisters that are nineteen.

So there is a big gap between us that can create fighting with our little sisters. Well, this car ride was different. I do not think I remember us fighting even one time throughout the whole drive. This was definitely a first. It felt so harmonious and I felt so loving and unified with my family. We were able to talk and laugh and have a good ride.

This student reported that it was her dad that took the lead in building a non-contentious event. She commented several times how good it felt to have time with her family that she loved so much. The opposite of contention is not the absence of contention. I think of harmony as being the opposite of contention. Take a look at Doctrine and Covenants 121:41–46 again. These verses give us an excellent constitution for relationship harmony. Starting with verse forty-one, it says that we should try to influence one another by using persuasion, long-suffering, gentleness, meekness, and love unfeigned. Let's take a careful look at each of these words.

First, the virtue of harmony only happens when we use *persuasion* with our children. Notice in the toilet-cleaning family example above that there were still high expectations for routines, but that they were able to get the job done and still promote a sense of unity and harmony.

A key word in D&C 121:41 is "persuasion." The word persuasion means resolve a disagreement by discussion. It also means to "win over" someone or win his or her approval. Another word for *persuade* is *convince.* Two people have two different ideas of how to solve a problem or what should happen next; they struggle together and present their ideas and a decision is made to either pick one of the possible ideas, or in that struggle, a new idea emerges that both can live with.

Harmony is about that kind of exchange. As our children become teenagers, our relationship with them has to be built on persuasion instead of control. Of course, I am not suggesting that they be allowed to do whatever they want if the two of you can't agree. Occasionally, there are some issues that you will, at the end of the day, have to agree to disagree on. And since you are the parent, you do have to be able to say, "In this case, we are going to solve this problem in the following way."

Choose carefully which issues you will be firm on. For example, you have every right to draw a line the sand about drug and pornography use. Our children knew that in our family, the family rule was you went to church. It was a clear rule, sometimes challenged, but usually followed. There were times they didn't want to go and times when some refused to go. But they knew the rule and as they got older (ages 17–18) that decision became more and more up to them.

Back to the story of Justin told earlier in the chapter, would you be willing to entertain a situation within which you said to a seventeen-or eighteen-year-old, "We want you to go to church. You know how we feel about it and it is a family rule. However, in the end, you are the one who has to decide."? The following JOT asks you to comment on that situation. What are your thoughts?

JOURNAL OF THOUGHTS
Do they have to go to church?

After reading the story of Justin not wanting to go to church and the discussion of contention versus harmony (especially with the idea of persuasion in mind), what are your thoughts? Should the parent allow a seventeen-year-old to make the decision to not go to church, or is it the parent's job to enforce the standard and insist the child go? If you pick "insist they go" as your answer, what is your next step if they refuse and say, "I'm not going—and you can't make me"?

_____

_____

_____

_____

_____

_____

Discuss your response here with your spouse or a friend. Find out their views and compare them with yours. Does your view stay within the bounds of building harmony, or are you tempted to move more toward compulsion?

_____

_____

_____

_____

_____

_____

Another focus in Doctrine and Covenants 121 is *long-suffering.* Long-suffering evokes the idea of patience, forgiveness, forbearance, and enduring a troubling situation with calmness. You may become provoked by your teenager—don't we all? Our job as fathers is not to become emotionally reactive, defensive, and over protective of our own delicate inner-self. Again, we sometimes miss the mark on promoting harmony because we feel attacked, and we are tempted to cover our own sins and feelings of inadequacy.

In fact, it is common for us as parents to feel attacked by the events within our homes. If our children are not doing what we think they should, it makes us look bad, we have the sense they are missing out on life's most important missions, we fear for their spiritual safety, and we worry about their actual physical safety. All of those are worthy of our worry. But our best chance at finding a way to solve these issues is promote harmony and avoid the ugliness of contention.

Gentleness is next. Being gentle in our interactions with others is about the disposition or tone we bring to the situation. The harmonious approach is to bring a tone of peace, kindness, and an attitude that is free from harshness or violence. Some synonyms for gentleness are *non-abrasive, soft, soothing,* and *tender.* The opposite and damaging side of this idea ties into the notion of control and compulsion. These words include *caustic, coarse, harsh, rough,* and *scathing.* Harmony, is built on a foundation of patience and gentleness. It is also has an element of *meekness* according to Doctrine and Covenants 121:41. Being meek doesn't mean we are wimps, submissive, and deficient in courage. The dictionary definition lists meekness as "enduring injury with patience and without resentment." When we are meek, we are modest in our response to others and are unpretentious. The opposite of being meek is to be arrogant, conceited, imperious, superior, and uppity.

In that same sentence of Doctrine and Covenants 121, the term *love unfeigned* is used. The word *unfeigned* simply means "authentic." If we feign our love to another it means we are manipulative, insincere, hypocritical, two-faced, deceitful, and duplicitous. The harmonious strategy in family leadership is to have the meekness, patience, and forbearance to let the Spirit do its work[50] and avoid strategies that chase the Spirit away.

So, according to Doctrine and Covenants 121:42 harmony is

about kindness and pure knowledge (think of the strokes of ideas from the Spirit) and using these tools without *guile*. A person who is "without guile" is not necessarily a person who is soft-spoken. Instead, a person without guile is not crafty and full of deception. A "non-guile" person is one who is transparent and honest.

Reproving betimes with sharpness is another phase used in Doctrine and Covenants 121; a prominent definition for *sharpness* is clarity or preciseness. *Reprove* means to correct, and *betimes* usually is defined as *speedily*—not *occasionally* as it has come to be defined more recently.

So a harmonious approach to solving life's struggles is to correct problems speedily and promptly using clarity, precision, and patience with a transparent and authentic heart.

Building Harmony and Avoiding Relationship Toxins

How do we teach our teens to embrace a more harmonious family lifestyle and decrease the contention? Like any of the virtues discussed in this book, there isn't a quick, easy fix. Of all the virtues talked about in this book, this one may be the most difficult to teach. That is particularly true if contention has been a significant element of your interactions with your teen(s) for an extended time period.

To begin, carefully and objectively assess how much conflict is happening in your family. Spend a few days or so keeping a conflict diary (see activity below) and try to be as objective about your assessments as possible. Being stealthy is important in this assignment. If you announce to the family that the month of September is going to be the *We-Are-Not-Fighting-Anymore* month, you will only make things worse. As I said earlier, most people don't want to be a part of anyone's "program" of change.

Assessing conflict and contention. In the Flourishing Families Project, every year we ask parents about what types of topics trigger conflict in their homes. In Wave III, the children in the study were about fourteen years old. We asked dads about the kinds of topics that generated conflict with these teens. The table below compares the differences between the teens in Seattle and those in Utah County, of mostly LDS families.

Before you look at that table closely, read down the left-hand side and mark the three topics that are most likely to generate struggle or contention in your home. Think of your teen or teens in this regard. If possible pick the child that is closest to age fourteen.

TABLE 3
Comparison of LDS and non-LDS dads' responses to conflict topics

Topics	Seattle	Provo
Money	37%	37.5%
Grades	41%	49%
Friends	12.5	19%
Free time	40%	55%
Curfew	10.5%	21%
Chores	51%	67%
School activities	13%	16.5%
Family time together	22%	26%
Alcohol use	3%	2.5%
Drug use	1%	2%
Tobacco	1.5%	3%
Clothing	15%	16.5%
Media use	24%	33.5%
Church	10.5%	9.5%
Sib fight	41%	60%
Dating	3%	4%
Attitude/respect	37%	49%
Discipline	26%	33%
Eating habits	26%	30%
Lying	11%	15%
Talking back	19%	24%
Rule breaking	16%	22%
Trouble at school	6%	6%

The chart above shows areas of conflict and score comparison between the Seattle (non-LDS) sample of families and the Provo (LDS) sample. The chart shows what percent of dads said that topic was a problem they were having with their teenager. The first thing to notice is that LDS dads' reports of conflict are, with almost all topics, higher than the non-LDS. I was surprised at this finding. I wonder if these LDS dads had higher expectations for their children, if the higher numbers of children in LDS homes creates more conflict, or if LDS dads are less tolerant of conflict and, therefore, are more likely to rate it as severe. The truth is we have no truly objective way of telling from this table if LDS families have more conflict than non-LDS, but as with several other measures of conflict between parents and between siblings, there is at least as much conflict in LDS homes as in non-LDS homes. And, frankly, I am a bit disappointed in that. Keep in mind that our sample of LDS homes is not representative of all LDS homes—it is just a snapshot of LDS families in Utah County. However, even when I look at the data of the thirty or so LDS families we polled in Seattle, the data aren't much different.

According to dads, the items that generate the least conflict in homes (LDS or non-LDS) are drug, alcohol, and tobacco use, along with dating issues. This points to an important idea in understanding how to work with teens about conflict. The topics seem to change as they get older. We have noticed in our research that the conflict dads report with younger teens (age twelve or so) mostly center on chores and other events within the home; as teens get older the topics shift to events located outside the home. And that means as they get older, dads and moms have less and less input in what is happening.

Next, the big topics in both samples were grades, chores, sibling fighting, sassing, and what the teen does with his/her free time. Sound familiar? One take away from this table may be that you find that your struggles are not that much different from everyone else. The typical family with teens is struggling to get their teen to live in the family as a helpful and responsible family member. Sometimes teens see their job as moving away from being told what to do. They don't care much about yard work and may not even really see the long-term big picture about grades. They may be more interested in friends, who is winning *American Idol*, texting, and paying attention to the latest trends. They are also, based on our table here, frequently annoyed by a younger sister or brother who is rummaging through her drawers and being a pest. Does any of this sound familiar? That your teen is displaying these kinds of "rebellious" expressions is pretty normal. She is starting the process of moving out, finding a partner, and shaping her own life. That is her job. And you will only make things worse if you try to derail that. You may be able to slow it down and keep her movement in those directions to a dull roar, but if you try and keep her your eleven-year-old princess, nothing good will come of that strategy.

Other teens may be contentious at this stage because they are not doing well with friends, they are embarrassed about how they look, unsure of their ability to make friends, or they feel like a failure at school. You can help in this regard, but it takes time, investment, and gentleness. Our knee-jerk reaction when a teen is pushing back, sassing, teasing siblings, not doing chores, and so on is to pull back and turn up the volume on keeping them in-line. In reality, in most cases an opposite strategy would work better. We need to find ways of connecting—not pulling-back and we need to help them make good decisions instead of trying to make the decisions for them.

Heal thyself. You probably could have guessed that a first step in teaching the virtue of harmony and decreased contention is to practice both of those attributes yourself. The following exercises were designed to last about one month. During the first week, prayerfully reread Doctrine and Covenants 121 with a special emphasis on those last verses that have been highlighted here. Record your thoughts and ideas as you read, cross-reference, ponder, and observe. The observing part is your anthropological self "visiting your own family." For several days, stand back and just observe what is going on. Take note of the sequences of interaction. Who says what to whom? When do they say it? When are contentious events breaking out?

Two-week daily diary. It is important to figure out how much conflict or contention is happening during a typical two-week period. Family therapists look for recurring patterns of behavior and interaction. Most of family life is kind of like a Shakespearean play. That is, everyone knows their parts and knows when to fall down and howl if someone touches them; another person knows when they are supposed to jump in and join someone in an argument; yet another person's job is to step at just the right time and send people off to neutral corners. If you are like most of us, you probably haven't paid much attention to these rule sequences. We use the word *rule* to indicate that it seems like families have gathered in the living-room and all agreed to follow a certain pattern when something happens. Here is an example of a rule sequence in my family when I was growing up:

This little "play" would happen at mealtime when everyone was there. Let's use breakfast as an example. My brother Dan is seven years younger than me, so when I was a senior in high school he was ten—a pesky ten-year-old that wanted nothing more than to have his older brother pay some attention to him.

I am minding my own business at the table—probably quiet and giving one-word answers to my mother, who is trying to pump me for information about what is going on at school or with a baseball practice that afternoon. She is getting irritated because she isn't getting much from me.

Dan reaches over and pokes me.

I look at him with a special look that says, "If you do that again, I will kill you and bury your body where no one will find it."

Dan doesn't pick up on the warning.

My mother pries deeper about school and the schedule.

Now my dad joins in and reminds me that the money I am making from my part-time job has to go to all my expenses, and he is not paying for extras this month. "Fine," I say in a contemptuous tone.

Dan takes this opportunity to "spill" the sugar on my cereal. It is done skillfully and at the right moment—no parents are looking.

I slug Dan.

He falls to the floor, howling like someone is removing his appendix without anesthesia.

Mom: "Why did you do that? Why are you always picking on Dan?"

Dad fights back. "Didn't you see that, Barb? Dan was asking for it."

Mom: "Why are you always siding with Randy—he is always picking on Dan and making his life miserable."

Dad: "You don't see the whole picture—you never have."

Mom: "Ralph, you are such a dummy."

Dan has long since stopped howling and is eating his cereal. The final line in this morning's drama is when my mother says, "Ralph, you are such a dummy." Dan smiles. And I leave out the back door—it probably slams a bit harder than usual.

That is the kind of cultural anthropological work I want you do for at least two weeks. Try to uncover the one-act plays that lead to trouble. Try and track conflict incidences back and find out where and when they started. It doesn't really help to try and find who is to blame. That is a waste of time. The point is to try and find the repeating sequences. You won't have much luck stopping conflict if you don't understand how these three to five minutes one-act plays work in your family. It may be helpful to give these a name so you can keep track of them. For example, I have labeled the above play, *The Case of Dan Needing His Big Brother—To Slug Him*. He really did need me to give him any kind of attention even if it was painful attention. Sorry, Dan; I should have been a better brother.

Investing in the moment—picture of cell-dad. Another key to decreasing kerfuffle before it becomes contention is to spend the time you are at home fully involved in home and not be distracted by other intrusions. It could be that children may be working on their three-minute dramas as a way to get you (or your spouse) to pay more direct attention to them. Take a look at the photo I took recently.

This dad is asking for trouble. **Warning:** *when you are with your family, be with your family.*

Becoming an intentional and invested dad means having significant amount of time with your family when they know that your complete attention is on them. We are moving quickly to a national level policy on distracted driving. Talking on cell phones and texting while driving can kill—and talking on phones and texting while you could be interacting in special and even ordinary moments is another way you can kill a relationship. The message the dad in the photo is potentially sending is that his "real" life is somewhere else and his family group is a necessary burden and obligation. For decades we have been able to conduct our business without the addiction of the electronic pacifiers hanging around our necks. We have come to believe in the last very few years that unless we are answering emails and texts every waking minute of the day, gravity will cease to exist. Okay—enough of the soapbox.

Sequence interruption—the 90-percent rule. Once we become attentive and invested in our families and do the work of identifying the sequences of the daily dramas, we can begin interrupting those sequences and actually changing the ways family members interact for the better. The 90-percent rule says that if we are attentive in our families, we can predict about 90-percent of what is going to happen next. You know with fairly high certainty that later today there will be daily dramas about certain topics. Is it Wednesday and tonight is Mutual? Are there any recurring dramas about Mutual? Are you having dinner together tonight? Did people go to school today and you know (because you are a with-it dad) that there was a math exam today? Most of what happens in life is not news to anyone. Mostly we go through the same issues, same patterns of interacting, and same dramas.

Teaching Children to Avoid Relationship Toxins

The following are four strategies that will help you teach your children how to avoid contention. Each of these ideas can be easily converted into a family home evening lesson and also are important Personal Father Interview topics.

1. Wag more, bark less. Probably my favorite bumper sticker of all times is the one that simply says, "Wag more, bark less." I am sure you have heard the old adage about first impressions. It is important to teach children that the first impressions concept is not only important for the first time we meet someone—but also for the first time we see someone each day. A key to managing conflict is to teach children to "wag" when they approach a family member. That is, if a person comes home from school and the first thing out of their mouth is a tirade about a teacher, complaints about a test, and how much they hate Jessica, then the rest of the day will not go well. First impressions happen each and every time we encounter someone. The tone we bring to that conversation each time is read by the other person.

2. Avoid trigger words that prompt contention. There is a long list of words that family members can be taught to use that will decrease the chances they will hit a trip-wire and cause a blow-up with another family member. Some words we use are by their very nature competitive and provoking.

Control talk is about influence and change. When we praise, lecture, direct, or request things from family members we are using control talk. Parents often supervise their children, monitor their activities by asking where they have been, and teach them about math at the dinner table while doing homework. All of these activities are control related. Here are some examples of kinds of competitive control talk that tend to spawn contention:

Interruption. When we become impatient and controlling, we interrupt others. As you are doing your anthropological assessment, observe how family members actually talk to one another, and notice the frequency of interruptions. Are people allowed to finish their sentence—or do others jump in and finish sentences for them? Interrupting someone is a signal that you don't really care what they are saying; most of the time that is true. There are times when non-competitive flow of conversation almost requires a running exchange, and we interrupt to show we care and are following what the other person is saying. However, the toxic kind of interrupting, when it is competitive and nasty, almost always leads to more contention.

Non sequitur. Non sequitur is another type of communication that leads to trouble. The term *non sequitur* is a legal term that means that one thought doesn't follow from the previous. Here is an example:

Bernice: I was thinking it would be a good idea to go to the movie tonight.
Ron: What's on?
Bernice: There are several good movies on I would like to see. I especially
*   like the Muppet movie. How about that?*
Ron: Why do you like those kinds of banal silly movies about puppets that
*   talk?*
Bernice: I dunno, I just like 'em.
Ron: That's the problem with the way you approach life. You think that all
*   the problems of life can be solved by going to some silly movie.*

Do you see the problem and why this simple conversation has the high potential of turning competitive and contentious? Ron doesn't understand that Bernice is not asking for a lecture about how she sees life—she is asking to go out and have some fun. In other words, part A of the conversation is not even remotely connected to part B. As you teach your children this principle, create some dialogue that suits your family. In the weeks leading up to a lesson on competitive communication in a family night setting, listen for examples of non sequitur speech that you could use in a demonstration. Be careful not to humiliate anyone.

Lecturing. "I told you a thousand times to not slam the bathroom door. Okay—I want you to stand there and open and close that door fifty times correctly." Fight language often starts with a lecture. A researcher/therapist named John Gottman tells us that we should pay attention to the five to one rule. That is we need at least five positive non-competitive, non-lecturing, non-bossy, non-aggressive interactions for each time we offer a correction. You have to have money in the "relationship bank" before you bark. Remember—**if you wag more than you bark, your relationships will soar. If you bark more than you wag, you will likely start a war**.

Superlatives. Another way to start a good fight is to use superlatives. Here are a few examples.

*You **never** take a shower without turning the bathroom into a disaster.*
*You **always** take my clothes without asking me.*
*You are a **total** idiot*
*Why do you **constantly** talk like a baby?*

A superlative is a word that defines an extreme. They frequently come attached to the word "you." Teach your children that using superlatives is like waving a red flag in front of a bull. We use superlatives to overwhelm someone with an argument, "You never take out the garbage." That is probably an exaggeration, but we use extreme language to crush our opposition into getting the point. Most of us push back when pushed. Teaching children about the negative impact of these types of trigger words can help them avoid the contention. Teach them that a more effective thing to say, "I get irritated when the garbage driver comes and our cans are not out there."

3. Avoid censuring in public. Teach children that it causes trouble when we censure, criticize, or condemn others in public settings. Avoid airing grievances at the dinner table, FHE, and other family gatherings. Teach them that it is normal to have grievances but ineffective to air them to the whole group. By broadcasting them to everyone, the accused not only *has* to defend their actions but also save face. No one appreciates being called out with others looking on.

4. See with clarity, acting promptly, and showing forth an increase of authentic love. Teach children to go to the offender quickly, with clarity and love. I would suggest you find ways of role-playing examples of trouble in FHE. You will have plenty to choose from if you do your anthropological assignment for at least two weeks.

PFI: Love Your Brother/Sister

Start by listing the seven items below. Most of them are about problems; two of them are about positive interaction. The results you see here are from the FFP and show a comparison between LDS and non-LDS. Generally, LDS youth reported significantly more sibling conflict than our non-LDS sample of families. One reason is that there are more children per household; the demands on space, time, money, and parents' attention is more divided.

Have your teens rank each of these with regard to trouble that happens in your home. By ranking, I mean have them decide which one of these seems to be at the heart of most conflict and which is least. Then rank each of the other in-between items. Don't show the results of the research until they have done their ranking.

Sibling Relationship	Non-LDS	LDS
Starts a fight	46%	52%
Mad and angry	46%	51%
Push or hurt	30%	28%
Tease/call names	49%	47%
Take other's things	28%	28%
Show affection	36%	49%
Help soothe other	57%	70%

Next, have them relate an incident from the list that happened recently. Encourage them to tell the whole story about what happened. Try not to use this time together to lecture, correct, or make moral judgments about right and wrong. Just listen to the story and hear their side of the whole story. As the story finishes, help them find ways that they could have done something different to generate a different outcome. What could they do in the future?

Finally, have your teens commit to keeping a two-week diary about the quarrels, fights, and conflicts that happen.

In a follow-up meeting, have them talk again about the list of quarrels that occurred and have them elaborate on the outcomes and what could have been done differently. Your job is to listen and hear their side. Try hard not to jump in and fix it all. The point is to be a person who will listen. Ultimately your teens will have to find solutions without you there—guide them in solving these issues rather than trying to be the person with all the answers.

Teaching Harmony

Let's assume you are amongst the majority of parents we interviewed that have children who engage in sibling conflict. Welcome to the club of normal families. The list in the previous box gives you a pretty exhaustive list of the kinds of topics siblings generally fight about. Notice that the LDS teens in our sample reported far more soothing and shows of affection to their siblings than did the non-LDS teens. At the same time, however, they also reported significantly more reports of getting angry at their siblings and more reports that their sibling had started a fight with them.

There are several good reasons to take this topic seriously in your family. Two years ago, my colleague and former doctoral student, Alisa van Langeveldt, completed her dissertation on sibling interaction as a source of strength during crisis. In her research, we found several important findings. First, like many other studies done on this topic, we found that children who grow in homes where there is increased levels of sibling conflict also report high levels of anxiety, depressive symptoms, and increases in delinquent behavior. Dr. van Langeveldt didn't find the strong negative effects that many other studies have found, but there was plenty of evidence that sibling conflict mattered in important child outcomes.

I am not ready to claim that sibling violence and fighting causes those three negative outcomes; but there is growing evidence that many of those problems bundle together. Also, you can think of sibling conflict as an area you, as the dad, can specifically attempt to do something about. That is not to suggest that mothers can't join in this campaign. But I would suggest that this is one of those areas where dads can take leadership.

The key finding Dr. van Langeveldt found in her study of our Flourishing Families Project was that when sibling conflict was paired with high levels of family stress, the net effect was very problematic for the teens overall. Sibling conflict exacerbated the already negative effects of stress on hope. Let's say that differently. We have found in our research that high levels of family stress seriously dampens feelings of hope in children and is also implicated in increases in what we call "internalized problem behaviors." Internalized problem behaviors are such things as depression, thoughts of suicide, and a sense of worthlessness. Dr. van Langeveldt found that sibling conflict magnifies that effect. When there is family stress *and* higher levels of sibling conflict, the outcomes are pretty substantial in promoting risk for teens.

The findings from this study will be published soon and should be taken seriously. Addressing the problem of sibling violence is gaining attention in family studies and rightly so. Our estimate is that somewhere between 60–80 percent[51] of children are victimized by a sibling. The scale we use to measure incidence of sibling violence is a scale that goes from slapping, pushing, hitting with an object, and eventually to stabbing or shooting. When measuring these violent acts, we usually only count the incident when there is serious harm done—not just the ordinary cases of rough and tumble play. Verbal and emotional abuse by a sibling is also a serious problem in US families. Consider the following specific strategies to help you intervene in sibling problems. These strategies feature a specific application of increasing gratitude between siblings, teaching the principle of forgiveness when there is injury among children, and how to use the principle of sacrifice with someone who annoys you and may even be abusing you.

Showing gratitude. This may surprise you, but research shows that when there is sibling rivalry, it is almost always within the context of parent favoritism.[52] While children's reports of parent favoritism may not actually reflect the parent's preference of a child, the really important part is whether or not the child believes that a parent likes the other child more.

As you work to decrease sibling conflict and also work to have siblings become a resource to one another (for example, being helpful, loving, soothing, and a friend) teach the target child to notice and appreciate the strengths of the other child or children in your family. If the mountain of research on gratitude is correct, you should have a specific and powerful experience having the target child implement these activities.

Take the time in your Personal Father Interview to review their gratitude diary with them. Use the time to help them think of things they notice about their brother or sister. In other words, model for them what you think about the other children, and add in four to five items that you are grateful for.

Sacrifice. Virtue #5 can be used here as well. Use the basic sacrifice questionnaire with your child, but rewrite it so it reflects their relationship with Kyle. It might say something like: *How hard is it to give something up for Kyle that means a lot to me? It makes me feel good to do something for Kyle.*

In the sacrifice section, the main idea was that doing something for someone can change your view of that person. In a *Personal Father Interview* with your child, design a series of "interventions" that are led by the target child. He is coached on how to put together a "secret Santa" type of program—regardless of the time of year. These acts of service could be making Kyle's bed, doing a chore for Kyle, or helping Kyle with a project. Along with this principle, teach your child the value of becoming a "Stealthy Helper." The Stealth principle says that it works better to implement changes in families when they are unannounced and quietly done. Try to protect the anonymity of the child doing the sacrifice.

Teaching the principle of forgiveness—in this context. If your family is like most of us, siblings sometimes don't get along. In fact, there may have been, among your children, "egregious crimes" committed toward each other. It might be a good idea to use the information presented about forgiveness as you work with your children. Again, it probably isn't going to work to think that a wonderful FHE lesson on forgiveness will change how they act and feel toward one another. It will take planning and thoughtful strategizing on your part to make it happen. I suggested that one way to implement the forgiveness principle is to pray for someone you are having trouble with.

This activity would be an excellent one to work on with your children individually. Find somewhere private. Have a talk with them about the scripture that says we can learn to love others as we pray for them, even if we are having a fight with them (Matt 5:44). Maybe take turns having a special prayer about a sibling that is having a struggle with the target child.

After the prayer, read several scriptures with your child about the power of forgiveness. Try to avoid giving long sermons at this point; invite your child to show how these scriptures could work with regard to the family relationship problems they are having. Repeat. Remember to keep trying: being a Heartbeat dad means pumping good blood into your family system for months and years—not minutes.

Virtue #7: Persistence
Heartbeat Fathers Never Give Up and They
Teach Their Children How to Have Grit

Nothing can take the place of persistence. Talent will not; nothing is more common than unsuccessful men with talent. Genius will not; unrewarded genius is almost a proverb. Education will not; the world is full of educated derelicts.
—Calvin Coolidge. 30ᵗʰ President of the United States

WE LOVE STORIES OF PERSISTENCE. MEN AND WOMEN WHO persevered through difficulties and trials built Western civilization. We love stories like those of Abe Lincoln reading night after night by candlelight; he is usually portrayed in such mythic-like stories overcoming humble beginnings. In like manner, we love the stories of athletes who persist against great odds and win despite handicaps. One of my favorites is that of a baseball player named Jim Abbott.

Jim Abbott was born in 1967, without a right hand. That didn't seem to slow him down much. With the spirit of true grit, he taught himself at an early age to play baseball and football. Many know of his baseball career, but he was also an excellent quarterback in high school. He played for Flint Central High School as their starting quarterback. He recorded an outstanding baseball career at the University of Michigan leading the Wolverines to two Big Ten championships in the late 1980s. He was a starting pitcher for the United States during the 1988 Olympics in Seoul and took home a gold medal. He went on to play for ten years professionally. His teams included the New York Yankees, California Angels, Chicago White Sox, and the Milwaukee Brewers. He is even reported to have hit one-handed home runs during batting practice. Jim now delivers motivational speeches and works with the Special Olympics.

Men like Jim Abbott are brilliant examples for us all. However, the kind of grit and persistence I want to talk about is found in ordinary Heartbeat fathers. In recent years, I have come to know many men whose lives were never in the spotlight, but are true heroes with ever bit as much perseverance as Jim Abbot or even Abraham Lincoln. The difference is they were never featured in newspaper articles, or were never "Man of the Year" in *Time* magazine, never given a ticker-tape parade in downtown Manhattan.

Here is a story that exemplifies the kind of fathers that have and teach true grit. This story is about an ordinary dad who wanted to build a basement so his kids could have more bedrooms. He was not rich when it came to money; but he was rich in courage and strength. Grit is about folks who have long-term goals and don't need a daily reward to achieve that goal. They persevere through rain and snow, the good times and the bad, and stick with their goals even when there are substantial obstacles.

My friend Kevin told this story to me and I share it with his permission.

After their marriage, Mom and Dad made their home in Orem (UT). My dad decided to become an auto mechanic and was able to secure a Sinclair gas station franchise located in North Orem. There was a neighborhood grocery store next door to the gas station and the primary road leading to Provo Canyon made this a good business location. As our family grew, my dad and mother built a small house near the gas station. It seemed spacious and wonderful after living in a small trailer house and then an apartment. But in the next few years three more children were added to our family and the house seemed a lot smaller than when we first moved in.

The city of Orem is located at the mouth of Provo Canyon. This canyon was, no doubt, created by a great river that fed into the massive Lake Bonneville that is now called the Wasatch Front. At the perimeter of Orem, and especially on the west side, there are large deposits of sand but near where were we lived it was composed mostly of a heap of rocks. If dad was not aware of this geography, he soon became a student of it when he set his mind to a plan to provide more room for his growing family. He would dig the dirt out from under the house and finish off the basement!

For most people this would mean hiring a company with a Bobcat to dig a ramp to the basement floor level, brace the foundation, and then dig under the foundation. But this service cost about $1,500 at the time. Spending that kind of money was not practical for a young man with five kids, a new business, and a monthly mortgage. So dad had to use the resources he did have: he owned a small pickup truck, a pick, and a shovel.

Dad worked long hours at the service station. He opened at 6:00 a.m. and got home after 6:00 p.m. at night. Each day he would come home, sit on a chair by the door and remove his greasy shoes. He would then take a bath, eat supper, and many nights would be off to a church meeting. Such a schedule left little time for digging out basements. Dad found the only possible time available to devote to his project—the half hour each day he took off for lunch.

*It was a tedious process—one shovel at a time—and often, one rock at a time. The process was not ideal. Dad would fill the shovel and then throw it into a pile on the ground behind the house. From the level of the floor in the basement, it would take the full reach of the shovel handle to get the dirt up to the ground level as he tossed the shovelful through the small opening in the foundation. He would then shovel the dirt from the pile in the back yard into the pick up truck. Once the truck was full, he would drive to the dump and shovel it off the truck. He repeated this process each lunch hour for **ten long years**! By this time, he had dug out half of the dirt in the basement.*

As the boys got older, the space was sorely needed. Jacks were used to support the main floor of the house while the space immediately under the foundation walls was dug out in sections. Concrete was then poured underneath the old foundation to support the walls. Once the foundation walls were poured, the older boys moved into the makeshift basement. We now had a place to sleep but were still sharing just one bathroom. The family size had grown to nine and the pressure on the bathroom was intense. To make matters worse, if you were downstairs in bed, you had to go outside and upstairs to get to the bathroom on the main floor. This was inconvenient in the summer and brutal in the winter.

For the last part of the digging, Grandpa showed up one day with a

177

tractor that had a bucket on the front. The boys now helped with the digging, throwing the dirt into the lowered bucket. The bucket would then be raised and dumped into the pickup, and we would gladly volunteer to take the dirt to the dump. Using a jackhammer, we eventually cut a window through the foundation wall to make access quicker. This process took another three years for dad and us boys to complete.

Kevin ends his story with the following note.

I've read stories about great men. I have read stories of men who were prisoners of war, stories of men who overcame much adversity to achieve great things. There are plenty of stories of perseverance, endurance, and commitment. None of these were written about my dad. But as I reflect on his commitment to serve God, his devotion to providing for our family, and perseverance in completing the basement (and many other jobs like it), I can find no heroes greater than him. I wonder what he was thinking as he dealt with the monotony day after day, when his muscles ached, when the task seemed futile? How many times did he want to quit? How often did it all seem hopeless? But, whatever obstacles he faced, he saw it through to the end. I don't need sports heroes or war heroes or even scriptural heroes to give me hope, strength, and courage. I need only to look to my dad.

There are three themes in this story that I want to focus on here. According to Kevin, he doesn't remember there being any big announcements in the family about digging the basement, it wasn't part of a ward quorum project nor was there a community celebration when it was finished. Kevin's dad also didn't make it a mandatory element of everyone else's life. Second, as I talked with Kevin about digging the basement, it wasn't billed as a work-camp project. Occasionally, I hear of fathers who get an idea, like making a basement, and they turn the family into prison slaves to get some long-term project done. The following story is such an example. In this story, the father wants to dig a basement, but instead of leading the way himself, the boys in the family were pressed into a work-gang each summer for five years. This story was told to me by a BYU student a few years ago, and I use it here with his permission.

Paul[53] completed his family analysis paper, but it came in late. When he came to my office, he was visibly upset. I have a special feature of the family analysis papers: if the student has written sensitive descriptions and ideas in the paper, then they can bring it to me personally and have me grade it without it going through the hands of my teaching assistant helpers. I was saddened as he began to tell me the story of his father and the many years of emotional abuse he and his siblings had suffered.

Paul said that one of the key things his dad thought he should teach his boys was to work and be persistent at a job even when you didn't like it. That beginning didn't sound like a problem to me. But as he began to tell the story about how his father pressed him and his brothers into a "work-gang," as he called it, I began to blanch a little. Starting the first morning when school was out for summer, the boys (beginning at age seven) would begin the day taking baseball practice at 5:00 a.m. The father would hit grounder after grounder for at least two hours until 7:00 a.m. Then at home, they would have a quick breakfast, after which they would be shown the work for the day that consisted mostly of digging. In their rather large lot, there was a space that had been allocated as the lot for a second home that was to be built and sold by the father.

The boys would work on digging the basement hole for the very large house every day for five to six hours, by hand. They were given a certain size of pile dirt they were to have in place by the time the dad got home. If they slacked off, the boys would have to double the size of that day's output—that day. So frequently, they would be digging, working the wheelbarrow up a makeshift ramp, and building their dirt piles late into the evening to fill their quota. The father never participated in this digging adventure. He was at work all day, and if the quotas were not filled, there were severe physical punishments metered out, even to the older teenage boys.

Each summer, for the five years of the digging, as school approached, the dad would then tell them that it wasn't going to work out to build a house that year and their job now was to fill the hole. They would then spend the month of August filling the hole and getting it ready for winter. The hole was dug, filled, re-dug, and re-filled for five summers.

Here are some problems with this model of teaching long-term planning and perseverance. First, compare this basement digging to the story of Kevin's dad. In Kevin's story, the father was the leader. He led by example and with love. Kevin's dad *showed* his boys how a long-term goal can be achieved even without money. On the other hand, Paul's father saw his job as prison-camp guard and his dad as "drill-sergeant," as Paul described it. When there was disobedience, out came the lash.

Second, the goal in Kevin's family was clear and real; they all could clearly see the end goal, and they knew it was a result that would benefit the whole family. In Paul's family, the goal was vague and ill-defined. Paul suspected that there was never any intention of building another house. According to Paul, the digging was designed to make people "learn the value of work" and "keep them boys outta trouble."

Third, the results were starkly different. In Kevin's family, the long-term feeling of affection for his father was everlasting. His children remembered him as a man of determination and grit. In Paul's situation, he could barely speak of the hatred and animosity he had for his dad. The digging incident (and many more examples found in his paper) left a deep hole in his heart where a father's love should have been. Paul's touching family picture made for class was simple. It was black and white with a simply drawn iron fist in the center. The motto of the family, as described by Paul, was "Arbeit Macht Frei." This is a German phrase that was posted at the entrance of the Nazi prison camps. It means ironically, "Work Makes One Free."

Paul reported in his paper that he doesn't speak to his father much. His parents divorced when he was an older teen. He has not made peace with the abusive and misdirected approach his father took. Kevin, on the other hand, recently read his story to his family at the bedside of his dying father. The adult children, according Kevin, wept openly as they thought about the great hero their dad had been to them.

What is persistence? According to a handbook on positive psychology,[54] persistence and perseverance are a bit different. Persistence is when we voluntarily complete long-term goals in spite of obstacles, difficulties, and discouragement. If I wanted to master the French language, I could persist at that even though it would be hard, it would also be fun. Perseverance is similar: the person who perseveres is someone who keeps on going even when there are obstacles and the process is not so fun.

Persistence and especially perseverance are highly valued in our culture and dads should be involved in demonstrating and teaching these valued ideas to their children. I created the handout on perseverance (show below) for my graduate students. One day several of them were in my office and they were commenting about how hard graduate school was for them. Their primary complaint was that some students seemed to have all the talent and skills and the work of getting a PhD seemed easy to them. As we talked, I suggested to them that even if some people were smarter (which I don't think they were) perseverance was the great *compensator*. That is, most of us can compete at activities at a higher level of performance than we believe we can. Persisting, practicing, and being industrious can compensate or fill in the gaps.

Hard work and **Perseverance**
are the great **compensators**

Only occasionally is an individual endowed with an unusual dose of a select talent.

For the majority of people, what creates *any* difference in outcomes is the person's willingness to:

persist at that which is difficult.

not let others inaccurately define who we are.

bounce back after a failure even when we don't want to.

remain teachable even when you think you have something mastered.

attempt new and different solutions when the old ways of doing things fail.

listen closely when others have an insight about you that you don't know about yourself.

appreciate that some activities are just not meant for you to do and be willing to move on to something else.

In short, find what it is you are meant to do—and do it

I very much endorse the idea that most of us are more alike than different. Only occasionally do you find someone with an unusual gift that is so immense that they only have to snap their fingers and a great idea or painting emerges. Even a quick look through the biographies of most men and women reveal that one of the key attributes that separates those who survive and make a contribution in their communities and those who become disaffected and struggle with finding any success, is their ability and drive to keep on trying.

I hasten to add that persisting doesn't mean that anyone who really wants to do something can eventually do anything. For example, most of us are never going to play center-field for the Yankees no matter how persistent we are. We all have limitations and different strengths. In addition, we are born into family community situations that can influence how we do in life. I think some parents do harm when they tell their children "If you just try hard enough, you could be anything you want." That just isn't true. On the other hand, we don't want to shatter the dreams of a twelve-year-old who believes he can be a pitcher for major league baseball. The skillful dad helps his children learn about guided perseverance. Instead of telling children they can be anything they want, a better storyline is helping children persist with talents and interests they have been given and find out what they are the best at.

Notice that perseverance statement is also having grit to know when to fold and walk away. I have known several people in my life who were not getting anywhere with their mindless persistence. They didn't know when to stop and walk away from a task that was not going to pay off.

There are at least two other elements of perseverance that should be noted here. First, the research on industriousness tells us something very simple but powerful. When teens have positive experiences with being industrious and are developing the virtue of perseverance, they are more likely to be industrious in the future. In particular, research indicates that doing activities when there is a reward associated with that activity works to encourage future effort and industrious behaviors. Over time, when a person is working hard at something (maybe there was some kind of initial reward associated with it—like $5) the worker begins to discover reward in actually doing the task. The task becomes rewarding; the success of being successful becomes rewarding.[55]

In like manner, we can inadvertently teach kids to be lazy. If we reward mediocre behavior and they receive the prize for little effort, we teach them to be less industrious and self-motivated. A good example of this is the Pine Wood Derby Race in Cub Scouts. In my experience, the intention of some leaders is well-meaning: they don't want anyone to be disappointed. However, the unintended effects of giving out "participation awards," even in the face of poor effort, are counter-productive. By giving everyone a prize, we can create a false sense of completion and success.

By the same token, it doesn't work well when the Pine Wood Derby turns into a competition between fathers to show off *their* ability. I saw a dad once who had spent countless hours shaping a racecar at his place of work (a local body shop), the child had barely participated in it, but the car won—and it was really beautifully and professionally painted. That seems counterproductive to me.

In fact, the research team found that these types of misplaced efforts by dads (like the professionally painted race car) can create a sense of entitlement and learned-helplessness. Learned-helplessness is a true disease: the person has learned, often in their teen years, that effort isn't particularly rewarding. They learn someone will step in at the last minute and fix their race car, do their homework for them, complete their Eagle project for them, and help them with all their applications to college.

In a recent poll in one of my lower division freshman classes at BYU, I asked them to hand in a report of how many times in a typical day they were required to check-in with their parents (usually the mother) or the parent checked in with them about assignments, what they were wearing, if they went to class, or if they were planning on going to FHE that night. About 36% of the class said that they were in contact with a parent more than three times per day about such issues. Many commented that they were required to check in between nearly every class and report back on what assignments they were given and how class went.

The following cartoon tells it all. The "good mother (or father)" believes that by helping—whether it be a race car for Cub Scouts or the weight-lifting example above—actually spoils efforts to teach the long-term effects of learning about the virtue of perseverance. As teens get older, it is their job to do the heavy lifting and build their muscles—it isn't about the product, it is about the process of growth and becoming.

"Let me help you, dear."

So, with those thoughts in hand, what is it that a dad could do to teach his children to work well, enjoy the struggles of life, and persist at the good things of life even when it was difficult? And how would an effective father teach those skills without turning his home into a prison compound? Heartbeat fathers try to instill a sound work ethic in their children and the ability to set goals and see those goals materialize without standing over them with a whip.

Assessment. First, let's examine some ratings parents made about their children's level of perseverance. In the Flourishing Families Project, we asked parents to rate their children on a number virtues and one of those was persistence. To get an idea of how persistent your child is compared to other parent's assessment of their teens answer the following questions:

Use the following: 1=Very much unlike him/her, 2=Unlike him/her, 3=Neutral, 4=Like him/her, 5=Very much like him/her.

___My child never quits a task before it is done.
___My child always finishes what he/she starts.
___My child is a goal-oriented person

___My child finishes things despite obstacles in the way.

___My child does not give up.

___My child never gets sidetracked when he/she works.

___When my child makes plans, he/she is certain to make them work.

___When my child gets what they want, it is because he/she worked hard for it.

Total Score—Add the individual score from above and divide by 8.

Here is what we found in our sample of nearly seven hundred teens. Notice the differences between the LDS and non-LDS sample and between boys and girls. A low score here for LDS boys is about 2.4 and a high score is 4.0. For girls, a low score is 2.6 and a high score is 4.3. Anything above a 5 or so for either would be a very high score.

	Boys	Girls	Total
Non-LDS	3.0	3.4	3.2
LDS	3.2	3.5	3.4
Total	3.1	3.4	

When it comes to perseverance the main difference is not between LDS and non-LDS. LDS teens (average age here was about fifteen) were slightly higher in perseverance according to their parents' ratings. There were gender differences: boys were rated as having lower perseverance than girls. This difference was not statistically significant, but, as you can see in the table, it was a consistent and a clear trend. Girls are generally more mature than boys, tend to be more focused, report more hope, and probably are generally favored by their parents over boys. In a recent study completed by my colleague Laura Walker and me,[56] we found that when fathers where more authoritative (they were firm without being harsh) and the teen scored higher on persistence, they (the teen) were much less likely to also report delinquency, they did better in school, and their parents were also more likely to report that they were kinder to others (pro-social behaviors). There also seems to be a connection between adolescent persistence scores and reported optimism. Kids who were seen as sticking to a task, getting hard things done, and completing long-term goals were more positive about their world.

PFI: How Would You Teach Persistence?

Jot down here ideas you have about how to teach your teen to stick with projects longer and be more persistent. During your interview with your teen, explore the ideas of this section.

_____

_____

_____

_____

_____

_____

The following is a distillation of twelve ideas that seem to recur in the research about persistence. Before we begin with those twelve ideas, take a few minutes and jot down your ideas of what you think you could do to enhance your child's persistence score and to conduct a Personal Father Interview about this topic.

_____

_____

_____

_____

_____

_____

Twelve Guidelines for Teaching Persistence

1. Help them do things. Think of the story of Kevin's dad. In that important lesson, Kevin's dad led the way by working first and then including his boys. It doesn't work very well to say to a teen, "Go out and dig a hole." It works much better if the teen understands the overall goal and knows you believe in the outcome enough to be there working along side him/her.

2. Help your teens find what they are good at and how they can contribute to society in a meaningful way. It is less helpful to decide in advance what you think is best for teens and then manipulate and move them toward something they may not want to do. Of course, there are some goals in life you may think of as not negotiable. But even with those goals, do what you can to make the outcomes a shared venture instead of something you want and they don't.

3. Be willing to have Personal Father Interviews with them on a regular basis during which you help them review how the week went, help them find and set new goals and help them feel the reward of self discovery. In previous chapters there have been specific Personal Father Interview assignments. The same is applicable here. I haven't made a special feature for that Personal Father Interview because in this case the PFI times together have to be built and structured by you and your child. Those times together need to occur several times per month where you discuss how things are going with the goals that have been set.

4. Help them be able to stop something with honor. If something isn't working well, help them find a way to turn their energy to another task without resorting to the mistaken idea that once you start something you have to finish it, or you are a failure in life. If football isn't their thing and it becomes clear that they don't like it—help them let it go in a way that saves face. They need to know you aren't disappointed and think they are a failure if they don't want to continue with ballet.

5. You have to persevere at teaching them perseverance. This is not a one-time lesson. If you do, you will create harm. They will feel the sting of failure and then will not want to continue.

6. Start off with easy forms of persistence. That is, find something that is easy to complete that you know he/she wants to do. Maybe it is something simple like beginning to play the piano. Another possibility is something concrete that has a beginning and an end like building a model or completing a project for school. A good example are the projects and sub-projects found in large selection of merit badges for scouts and the possible activities found in the Young Women's Personal Progress program.

7. Make sure that the overall larger project is broken down into smaller manageable projects. If you simply say, "You need to get an A in math this year—or else," you will decrease the chances of them understanding the process of being persistent. Persistence is about doing small shovelfuls of work each day. Help them find and complete the small doable tasks on a daily basis. Since we live in an instant gratification world, this is difficult. Getting an A in math can't be solved by taking an aspirin.

8. Personal Father Interviews. I mention this again because it is so important that they know you haven't forgotten. You can show you care and love them by helping them refocus frequently. You may inadvertently drive them away by being a pest and an intrusive overbearing parent. They may believe you want them to complete an Eagle project because it will make you look good.

9. Showing gratitude. The ideas from the section gratitude will work here. During Personal Father Interviews, make sure that you tell them you care about them—but just as important, tell them directly about how you are grateful they are in your family. That means you will have to look for new things to be *specifically thankful* for each time. Example: *I was grateful last night when you gave Tyler a hug. That meant a lot to him.* If your PFI time is only about goals and productivity, it will send the wrong message.

10. Teach about sacrifice. Show them you care by sacrificing your time to be with them, work on projects, help with homework, and work on the next project for her Young Women's Personal

Progress. Also, include in your time with your teen planning times when you can do something together for someone else. As you build an attitude of sacrifice and commitment with your teen, they will be more likely to see the benefit of the things you are trying to convince them are worthwhile.

11. Show them you can be a part of their life without using power, compulsion, domination, or control. Building a sense of persistence is about inner direction—not direction that comes from external sources, like one's parents. If you are being a controlling, domineering, and compulsion driven parent, then this whole list of ideas will become quickly contaminated.

12. Don't start this list of ideas if you aren't serious. If you only do get involved for a few days or weeks and then give up—you will possibly create mistrust and distance. So pick something you can stick to. If you travel, set up regular times when you can talk.

Conclusions

I have one final thought. As I have been writing and thinking about the ideas in this book, it has become very clear to me the topics of sacrifice, persistence, forgiveness, expressing gratitude, and building a family based on harmony are joined together and connected. These ideas work because they come from the same source.

> Let thy bowels also be full of charity towards all men, and to the household of faith, and let virtue garnish thy thoughts unceasingly; then shall thy confidence wax strong in the presence of God; and the doctrine of the priesthood shall distil upon thy soul as the dews from heaven.
> The Holy Ghost shall be they constant companion, and thy scepter an unchanging scepter of righteousness and truth; and they dominion shall be an everlasting dominion, and without compulsory means it shall flow unto thee forever and ever. (D&C 121:45-46)

In short, our primary theme throughout this book has been to teach children about God by trying to be more like God ourselves.

We should also be a constant companion with our children, and our insignia (scepter) should represent what we stand for and what is important. That scepter should be a staff and insignia of righteousness and truth. And we should promote those core beliefs without compulsory means. The beauty of that final thought is that it is guaranteed to work over the long haul. No matter how the results turn out in the short term, the goal is to be a beacon and ensign of truth without compulsion.

Endnotes

1. William J. Doherty, *The intentional family: Simple rituals to strengthen family ties* (New York: Quill, 1997).

2. From *A League of Their Own* (1992) Starring Tom Hanks.

3. M. E. Lamb, *The Role of the Father in Child Development* (New York: John Wiley and Sons, Inc., 1976).

4. M. Ainsworth, M. Blehar, E. Waters, & S. Wall, *Patterns of Attachment* (Hillsdale, NJ: Erlbaum, 1978).

5. John 13: 34–35.

6. Richard G. Scott, "Honor the Priesthood and Use It Well." *Ensign*, Nov. 2008, 44-47.

7. M.E.P. Seligman, *Flourish: A visionary new understanding of happiness and well-being*, (New York: Free Press, 2011).

8. This story was recounted most recently by Elder Dallin H. Oaks in the LDS General Conference Sunday Morning Session, October 1985. The original story can be found in "Our Spiritual Heritage," in Brigham Young University 1981–82 Firesides and Devotional Speeches, Provo: Brigham Young University Press, 1982, 138.

9. Matt. 6:21.

10. Neal A. Maxwell. "Swallowed Up in the Will of the Father." *Ensign*, Nov. 1995, 22.

11. Moses 4:1–5

12. Know This That Every Soul is Free, *Hymns*, no. 240.

13. M. A. Lamb, *Father's Role in Child Development* (New York: Norton, 2011).

14. J. H. Pleck, "Paternal Involvement: Revised conceptualization and theoretical linkages with child outcomes." In M. E. Lamb (Ed.), *The Role of Father in Child Development* (5th ed.) (Hoboken NJ: John Wiley & Sons, 2010).

15. R. L. DeBoard-Lucas, G. M. Fosco, S. R. Raynor, & J. H. Grych, "Interparental Conflict in Context: Exploring Relations Between Parenting Processes and Children's Conflict Appraisals." *Journal of Clinical Child and Adolescent Psychology*, 39(2), (U.K.: Taylor & Francis, 2010) 163-175.

16. R. D. Day, & L. M. Padilla-Walker, "Mother and father connectedness and involvement during early adolescence." *Journal of Family Psychology*, 23(6), (2009) 900-904.

17. Questions adapted from A. J. Hawkins, K. P. Bradford, R. Palkovitz, S. L. Christiansen, R. D. Day, & V. R. A. Call, "The inventory of father involvement: A pilot study of a new measure of father involvement." *Journal of Men's Studies*, 10(2), (2002) 183-196.

18. *The Family, A Proclamation to the World*. Published by the Church of Jesus Christ of Latter-day Saints. (Salt Lake City: 1995).

19. 1William J. Doherty, *The intentional family: Simple rituals to strengthen family ties* (New York: Quill, 1997).

20. Dallin H. Oaks, "Spirituality." *Ensign*, Oct. 1985, 61.

21. "Too Young to Be Sexy" found at http://abcnews.go.com/2020/

22. John Sutter, "Survey: 15 percent of teens get sexual text messages." *CNN Reports.* December 15, 2009.

23. Z. Eisenberg, "You cannot show a pregnant woman on television: I Love Lucy and the cultural making of the visible belly bump in post-World War II America." *Bershire Conference of Women Historians.* (2011).

24. US Census Bureau, National Center for Health Statistics, 2010. Washington DC.

25. P. W. Pruyser, *The minister as diagnostician: Personal problems in pastoral perspective* (Philadelphia: Westminster Press, 1976).

26. Aristotle, *Nicomachean ethics* (R. Crisp, Translation). Cambridge, England: Cambridge, University Press, 2000).

27. *Sunday Night Talks,* 2nd ed. (1931), 483.

28. Thomas S. Monson, "The Divine Gift of Gratitude." *Ensign,* Oct. 2010, 90.

29. Luke 17:11–19

30. M. E. McCullough, R. A. Emmons, & J. Tsang, "The grateful disposition: A conceptual and empirical topography." *Journal of Personality and Social Psychology,* 82, (2002) 112-127.

31. R. A. Emmons, and J. Hill, *Word of gratitude for the mind, body, and soul* (Radnor, PA: Templeton Foundation Press, 2001).

32. These items are from the McCullough et al. research above. They are part of a larger series of items used to assess gratitude and thankfulness.

33. F. B. Bryon, & J. Veroff, *Savoring: A new model of positive experience* (Mahwah, NJ: Lawrence Erlbaum, 2007).

34. This activity is based on the work of R. Emmons, & M. McCullough, "Counting blessing versus burdens: An experimental investigation of gratitude and subjective well-being

in daily life." *Journal of Personality and Social Psychology,* 84, (2003) 377-389.

35. Marion D. Hanks, "Forgiveness: the Ultimate Form of Love." *Ensign,* Oct. 1973, 20.

36. Smedes, *Forgive and Forget: Healing the Hurts We Don't Deserve.*

37. Handbook of Forgiveness, 2005.

38. Denham, et al., 2005.

39. Harris & Thorensen, 2005.

40. Fincham, Stanley, and Beach (2004, 2006, 2007).

41. All names have been changed in this story. And, the story is a composite story of several I have been involved in recently.

42. For articles related to sexting, start at the following website www.thenationalcampaign.org. Once at the website, type in "sexting" into the search feature.

43. Handbook of Forgiveness, 2005.

44. "Throwing the Book at O.J. Simpson; Fred Goldman Is Hot on the Tale of the Man He Says Killed His Son." *Washington Post,* Sept 13, 2007.

45. As with all stories in this book, the names have been changed and stories are used with permission.

46. Reported from the Online Etymology Dictionary, www.etymonline.com accessed 10-30-2011.

47. R. N. Bellah, R. Madsen, W. M. Sullivan, A. Swidler, & S. M. Tipton, *Habits of the heart: Individualism and commitment in American life.* (Berkeley, CA: University of California Press, 1985).

48. S. M. Stanley, H. J. Markman, M. St. Peters, & D. B. Leber, "Strengthening marriages and preventing divorce: New directions in prevention research." *Family Relations,* 44, (1995) 392-401.

49. Jeffrey R. Holland, "The Tongue of Angels," *Ensign*, May 2007, 16.

50. James 1:4. This scripture tells us that we need to cultivate the attitude of patience as we listen to the strokes of ideas that come to us. And, then act upon those in faith believing those ideas will work.

51. Kristi L. Hoffman & J. N. Edwards, "An integrated theoretical model of sibling violence and abuse." *Journal of Family Violence*, 19, (2004) 185-200.

52. L. J. Zervas & M. F. Sherman, "The relationship between perceived parental favoritism and self-esteem." *Journal of Genetic Psychology*, 155, (1994) 25-33.

53. Names have been changed to ensure anonymity.

54. C. Peterson & E. P. Seligman, *Character strengths and virtues: A handbook and classification.* (Oxford: Oxford University Press, 2004).

55. R. Eisenberger, "Learned industriousness." *Psychological Review*, 99, (1992) 248-267.

56. In press, Keep on keeping on, even when it's hard" Predictors and outcomes of adolescent persistence. *The Journal of Early Adolescence.*

About the Author

DR. RANDAL DAY WAS BORN AND RAISED IN THE NORTHWEST. HE served an LDS mission in England from 1967 to 1969. Dr. Day graduated from BYU in 1973 with a BS in speech and hearing sciences; obtained his master's degrees in 1974 from BYU in family science; was awarded a master's degree in child developmental from the University of Wisconsin in 1975; and finished his PhD from BYU in 1977 in family science andsociology. He is married to Larri-Lea Kissell, and they have five children and six grandchildren. He has taught at South Dakota State University and Washington State University and has been in the School of Family Life at Brigham Young University since 1999.

Dr. Day has numerous publications in the field of family science. His research interest primarily focuses on fathers in family life. He does research with men who are in prison and about to return home. His current focus is as a leader of the of Flourishing Families Project. This research project has reinterviewed seven hundred families in Seattle and Provo each summer for the last six years.

Dr. Day is a coauthor of the recent book entitled *Sacred Matters: Religiosity in Family Life*. He is an avid photographer and loves to play bluegrass guitar and old time rock-n-roll. He also loves to spend time with his children and grandchildren.